welcome to advertising!
now, get lost.

D1741952

OMKAR SANE

TRANQUEBAR

TRANQUEBAR PRESS
An imprint of westland ltd
571, Poonamallee High Road, Kamaraj Bhavan, Aminjikarai, Chennai 600 029
1 Floor, Praja Bhavan, 53/2 Bull Temple Road, Basavangudi, Bangalore 560 019
1 Floor, 3-5-1108, Maruthi Complex, Narayanaguda, Hyderabad 500 029
Plot No 102, Marol Coop Ind Estate, Marol, Andheri East, Mumbai 400 059
F-5, Okhla Industrial Area, Phase-1, Mezzanine Floor, New Delhi 110 020

First published in TRANQUEBAR by westland ltd 2009

10 9 8 7 6 5 4 3 2 1

ISBN 9789380032504

Cover design and Chapter Titles by Jezreel Sarah Nathan
Illustrations by Aindri Chakraborty

Typeset in Trebuchet MS by SÜRYA, New Delhi
Printed at Thomson Press

£15.99

welcome to wherever you are!

acknowledgements are overrated

I don't want to thank my parents. Frankly, they dismissed this as farcical.

I do not want to thank everyone who said it was silly to try it.

I do not want to thank my friends; they avoided me since I talked of nothing else.

I do not wish to thank anyone, in fact.

Except, everyone in advertising. It is they who made this book possible by making this their reality. Well, almost.

'I have written a book on advertising and I want your comments,' said a voice on the phone. 'Sure, which agency do you work for?' I asked. 'I don't work in advertising any more; I worked in an agency only for a few months.'

And he has written a book on advertising? I kept asking myself till I got the manuscript. As I raced to the last page I realised that people who have made advertising their lifelong career shouldn't write books on advertising. They tend to be self-indulgent, self-congratulatory, heavy with sharp insights and path-breaking strategies . . . all in hindsight.

This book is a sharp-witted look at the advertising industry as it really is. It tells you why most of the time advertising agencies work so well and advertising doesn't.

The book is so realistic that you worry when you laugh at most of what's inside. All I can say is, with this kind of edgy writing skill, I'm glad Omkar wasn't in advertising when I was.

I have no idea why Omkar wanted me to write a comment on this book. Unless of course he wanted a comparative reckoner to show how beautifully his own language flows.

My advice is, if you're in advertising, you must read this book. It's a mirror to your professional life that will make you laugh and . . . No, actually, it'll only make you laugh (advertising professionals don't have time to introspect).

And if you are not in advertising, you must read this book because you need to know what you're getting into (even if you want to get out as quickly as Omkar did).

The best thing I can say about this book is: 'I wish I had written it.'

BHARAT DABHOLKAR

A note on the book And Author, is Cyrus Broacha's Claim to Fame.

When Omkar Sane asked me to write a brief introduction to his book, I had only one question: 'Who is Omkar Sane?' Or, more importantly, 'What's an Omkar Sane?' And 'Was Omkar Sane the name of a religious cult I may or may not have joined under the influence of spirits on a weekend binge many years ago?'

However, after doing my research and investigations, I found out three important facts about Omkar Sane I'd like to share with everyone. A. Omkar Sane is a male. B. Omkar and Sane are two separate people. C. I once borrowed forty-four rupees from Omkar Sane to pay for a taxi and since I had not returned the money, this is his way of making me pay for it. Not just by writing an introduction but also by making me read his book. Twice!

Now let's delve into the Omkar Sane story.

To celebrate India's 1983 World Cup cricket win, Omkar was born in or around 1984 in a place called Goregaon. This is a suburb of Mumbai, many, many miles away from Calcutta. After securing well over 10 per cent marks in his school exams, Omkar joined the Sir J.J. School of Art where he was the last man to see Sir J.J. alive and taking a bath. His hobbies include photography, reading and eating. Of these he is most proficient at reading while eating, and intends to take that up professionally if this book sells less than two million copies.

His years of experience include five days at Ambience Publicis (ad agency), seven at Contract Advertising (they made him work Sundays there) and a couple of weekends at MTV (MTV used to be a music channel).

Now a word about his book. It's the best book I've ever read although I must add that after page 9 an acute attack of haemorrhoids rendered me unable to complete it. However, ad legend Prahlad Kakar (who has been in advertising since Mangal Pandey was a teenager) says it's a revolutionary piece of work second only to his own bestseller, *How to Cook a Fish on the Lakshwadeep Islands*.

Five reasons to buy this book
1. Omkar needs money
2. Sane needs money
3. Mr Kakar needs money
4. I need money (I even danced for it)
5. You need a laugh (Quick! The remote; put on the news.)

If you want to know more about Indian advertising read the book.

If you want to know less about Indian advertising, join it.

CYRUS BROACHA

The Foreword is written by a real writer called Gangadharan Menon

I hate reading forewords.

But I gladly agreed to write one for Omkar.

The reason is, anyone who has dared to pick up this book needs to be forewarned.

I have been too close to advertising. For close to twenty-five years.

So close that I have developed a blind spot.

Fortunately for Omkar, he came close to advertising. And then got out of it.

So his is an insider's-outsider's view.

Inside enough to know what's happening.

Outside enough to see the funny side of it.

Rarely would you find this point of view. With an edge chiselled to match.

So, enjoy!

GANGADHARAN MENON

should definitely not be skipped.

The Introduction

Advertising is a business dedicated to creating, planning and handling advertising (and sometimes other forms of promotion) for its Clients—businesses and corporations, non-profit organisations and government agencies. And the place where all this happens is called an Ad Agency. Ad Agencies produce single Ads or, more commonly, an ongoing series of related Ads, called Advertising Campaigns. Yes . . . and Nehru ruled Namibia.

No, seriously. It's about:
a. Free beer.
b. Casual clothes (casual to the point of being socially unacceptable).
c. Unshaven faces (they are considered cool and work as a perfect suggestion of the busy lives people in advertising lead).
d. Late nights—so many that your parents begin to consider adoption or letting out your room, which is fine, since you're:
   • Sleeping on the reception couch
   • Playing video games
   • Maintaining a healthy balance between both of the above
e. A worried dad.

An Agency is an absurdly cold place that doesn't charge you

any rent no matter how long you stay there, with uncomfortable chairs everywhere, except at the reception (the reception has the most comfortable sofa, probably to mislead youngsters coming for interviews about life in the industry, but nobody can tell), a hot receptionist whom only the HR manager has seen because she's usually on a lunch/tea break somewhere, leaving behind a thoroughly bored watchman.

It's a world full of people with colossal egos who act, talk and behave as if *they* came up with the force of gravity—or a cure for dandruff. (Yes, it's wrong to generalise, especially when only 99.9987 per cent are like that.) It's because they consider themselves special, doing what not many do for a living— playing cricket with a plastic bat and paper ball and calling it work, for instance. It's about people who essentially hate their job but have learnt how to look cool doing it, usually standing outside the office or with 'cool' posters pinned on their soft board.

Here are some pre-Advertising questions and their correct answers:

Q. What does Advertising mean?
A. We'll let you know when we find out.

Q. What is Advertising all about?
A. Are you sure your parents aren't reading this?

Q. What is a good time to join an Ad Agency?
A. Puberty.

Q. What are the qualifications for Advertising?
A. There are many. Education isn't one of them.

Q. Are there too many late nights?

A. Only if you get a good hand on the video game.

If you have a friend who is a part of this industry, there must've been times when you bumped into him at the bus stop in the morning (or maybe not, considering the late nights) and wondered what KIND of a life he leads—unshaven, in jeans, an unwashed T-shirt, sneakers or flip-flops. And that's just why many youngsters have begun choosing Advertising over prestigious, conventional jobs in fields like medicine (of the doctor-at-the-personal-clinic sort) or engineering or chartered accountancy.

Job	Doctor	Engineer	CA	Ad Guy
Day starts at:	Around 10 am	9.30 am onwards	9 am onwards	4 pm (on a bad day)
Work:	Usually fixed	Usually fixed	Usually fixed	Only between coffee breaks and cricket matches
Biggest challenge at work:	Examining someone's private parts	Fiddling with machines that want to blow up all the time	Going through files with numbers smaller than atoms	Saving your chair
Money:	Good	Good	Good	Are any kids reading this?
Job Hazards:	Contracting a contagious disease	Death or severe injury	Promotion	Sleeping on a chair instead of a sofa
What makes it worth it:	Saving lives	Building nations	Building corporations	Free beer

Some 'Test-Your-Advertising-Aptitude' questions:

Q. If you came to know of the ills of smoking, you would:
    a. Quit smoking.
    b. Try and get your friends to quit smoking.
    c. Smoke a cigarette; write an anti-smoking Ad in the hope of winning an award.

Q. You have an important meeting. You would:
    a. Pull out your best suit.
    b. Wear your best shirt and polish your shoes.
    c. Change your underwear.

Q. Early-in-the-morning to you is:
    a. 5 am; you practise yoga.
    b. 6.30 am; you jog.
    c. Noon.

Q. Late-at-night to you is:
    a. Past midnight.
    b. If you miss the last train/bus home.
    c. When the beer is over.

Q. Most important aspect of your job?
    a. Achieving targets.
    b. Making profits.
    c. Fighting to keep your chair.

If you've got all Cs, Welcome to Advertising! Now, Get Lost.

As the definition suggests, Ad Agencies provide solutions— bedding solutions for homeless employees, and solutions for Clients and other organisations. The Client is the person who puts up the money to create Ads for his organisation; Ads that he hopes will sell his product/service. It's something like betting on horses at the Derby, where the horses aren't even aware that it's a race. The Client, like the guy who's betting, is constantly tense and worried and the members of the Creative team, on the other hand, are the horses who think it

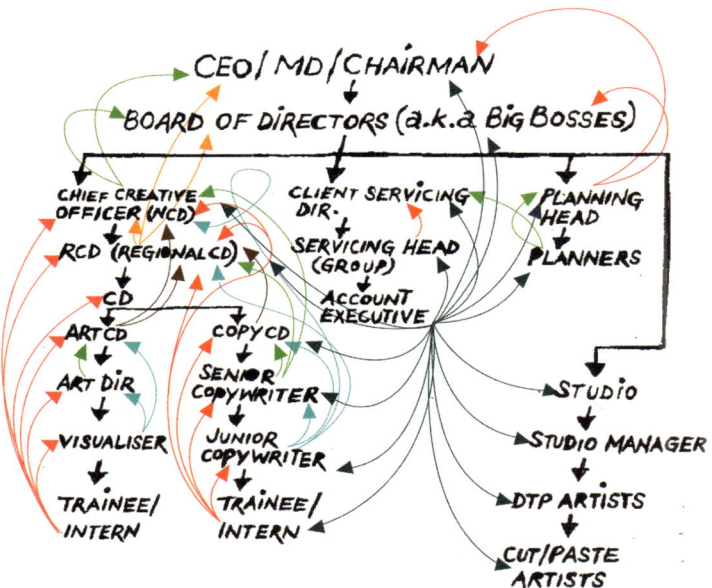

is some seventh grade science project. Unlike a school science project though, where you need a little fan and a canal with a bulb at the end, which is all very easy to get from the attic or the local hardware guy, getting Clients isn't easy. It's not like you open a place with a few computers, have a few guys and girls floating around in jeans and T-shirts, and Clients will walk up to you. No, you need more; a bed, for instance.

Winning a Client is like wooing a girl—you have to spend on her, impress her with flashy things she doesn't understand, pamper her, meet her unreasonable demands, be on your toes at all times of the day (and night) and massage her ego before she becomes yours. The only difference is that while the wooing is done by the interested boys themselves, Agencies hire freelancers.

And the process of winning a Client is called a Pitch.

the
pitch

A Pitch is called for by a Client when:

1. He isn't happy with his existing Agency. This usually happens when the Client visits the Agency and finds somebody fast asleep in the library or grown-up men playing cricket, fighting over a plastic ball.

2. The Client is new in the market and wants to launch a product/service and doesn't know who will make him look best in the market. And the best idea that they can come up with is to invite Agencies to come up with ideas for them.

3. The Client has made profits and, instead of distributing them amongst his hardworking employees who are responsible for the profits, he decides to spend on advertising his brand, hoping to increase the profits so that he can, no, not distribute them to his employees, but call the Agencies for a Pitch again.

Usually, all the groups in an Agency work on the Pitch as they make multiple Ads with different *routes* for the same Client.

Here's an example:

There's a Pitch for a large airline company. Each group tries to come up with a different route—not to be confused with the actual route that the plane flies on—to sell the airline to the airline itself. A route is nothing but a different way of looking at the same airline and its benefits—like a group of boys who lust after the same girl in a coffee shop for completely different reasons. Members of the Creative have to search and choose the best feature according to them. One group chooses to highlight the comfort the airline offers, another chooses its low fare, a third chooses speed, etc. Armed with these different routes, each group makes campaigns *only* on *their* assigned route.

Different routes are worked on:
1. To impress the Client by proving that Creative really thought about the product and left no stone unturned in finding ways to make it look good.
2. To avoid quarrels. There are already more important questions like 'Who gets to bat first?'
3. To avoid copying of ideas. This is appreciated only when the idea copied is from an outside source and wins an award.

The Pitch is one of the few things that unite everyone in an Agency as everyone sets their egos aside to work together. Others are:
a. Beer.
b. Do we need to get to b?

The actual Pitch is a very important, high-level and serious meeting attended by Senior Creative representing different Agencies that the Client has chosen to brief on the task.

Scene: A huge, expensive room with the important members of an Agency assembled in their best clothes (often, not noticeable to the naked eye, since it's just a change in underwear) waiting for the Client to arrive. After a long wait—sometimes for days—the Client arrives.

Client: Gentlemen, we all know why we're here.

Blank looks around the room.

Client: The competition is fierce. Consumer loyalty went out with the last century and it's difficult to keep someone stuck to your brand.

Blank looks turn to suppressed yawns.

Client: So, we need a new positioning, a new campaign, something that has never been seen, never been done, never been heard of in any market, in any country, except Iceland, since we don't expect anyone to go there in the near future. We need to break the clutter of the category, transcend all boundaries of possibilities. Synergise our benefits; increase our market share with some serious product differentiation by thorough research of the Target Market. And the only way to do it is with some analytical, conceptual thinking, downsizing losses with dynamic solutions that not only engage the consumer but also invite them to be a part of the growth of the brand. We need innovation, initiative and, above all, integrity. The bottom line is (*reaching a crescendo*) we need to think out of the box!

Creative (*whispers*): I heard him say 'integrity'. Are we in the right meeting?

Client: And that's why we need you. Let's see the campaigns a month from now. Let's see MY brand come alive!!!

After the brief, the top bosses travel back to their Agencies in the big cars thinking about what they can do.

Boss 1: Do you think there is merit in the Client?

Boss 2: Do you think he really knows what he's saying?

Boss 3: Any first thoughts?

Boss 1: No.

Boss 2: No.

Boss 1: How about you? Any ideas?

Boss 3: Yes, one.

Boss 1: Superb. What is it?

Boss 3: Let's hand it over to the juniors in the office. After all, they need to grow.

Boss 1: That's a lovely idea. But what will we do?

Boss 3: Supervise them. And then blame them if it falls apart.

Boss 1: But who'll break it to them?

Boss 3: The National Creative Director and the Creative Directors.

The National Creative Director has a lot of perks—a big cabin, a massive salary and a platoon of men and women to wash his luxury car. But with the perks comes the making of decisions—which car does he want washed first, which kind of chair is good, will his salary become obvious if his cabin is bigger than the office? When he's not making such important decisions, he's travelling, but spends nothing out of his own pocket, all trips being 'Official'. He is the guy who, at least in an ideal scenario, approves Campaigns and ideas, supervising the work of all offices of the Agency across the country; approving *only* the important Campaigns—the ones that require him to travel across the globe qualifying as important—and pushes others to work towards winning international and national awards for the Agency. The motive to win awards is to feature in fancy lists such as 'The Nation's Most Influential Creative People' drafted by journalists working for unpopular magazines. Featuring in such lists assures him:

1. Fame.
2. Money.
3. Do we still require the third?

A trainee working hard on a leaflet sees him only in two places—in the loo and from the bus window at the signal where he spots the NCD sitting in his luxury car.

There are some basic criteria one must meet to be the National Creative Director:

1. A paunch that can be hidden if you suck in your breath hard enough for it to show on your cheeks.
2. A firm belief that the paunch doesn't exist.
3. Knowing names of books you've never read, movies you've never seen, Ads you've never heard of and places you've never been to.
4. A perfected repertoire of profound expressions.
5. A big enough presentation that can go on till bladders explode.
6. The presentation should date back to, at least, the Indira Gandhi administration.

Above all, the most important attribute the NCD needs to possess is the 'The Art of Idea Conversation'—one which can be mastered over time, after sitting through mind-numbing, kidney-bashing, ass-torturing presentations.

Scene: The NCD's grand cabin. The Junior Art Director walks in, spending the first seven minutes gazing at all the framed awards, the *Award Annuals* (weighing thirty-four kilos each) and a twenty-one-inch laptop.

NCD: (*Turning around in his grand chair, he flashes a warm smile.*) Yes?
Junior Art Director: Sir, I have a new idea for an Ad.
NCD: (*Nodding approvingly*) Go on . . .
Junior Creative: We shoot this big car in a posh location next to a nice-looking building against a picturesque background . . .
NCD: You mean a Mercedes, like the one I have, beside (*thinking*) a canal, the one I showed pictures of from my last trip abroad (*clapping enthusiastically*) transposed against an

Edwardian building, the kind of hotel I stayed in on my last trip to London?

Junior Creative: (*Amazed, in an ecstatic voice*) Yes! Yes!

NCD: Go on.

Junior Creative: And you know a really . . . (*Making a flower vase with his hands*) in the balcony.

NCD: You mean a hot model, the kind we've used here (*pointing to a frame on his wall which is a poster from* Playboy *that he got because his letter got published in it in the seventeenth century or when Mr Hefner was young, whichever CAME earlier*).

Junior Creative: (*Vibrating with excitement*) Yes!

NCD: And . . .

Junior Creative: And a dude . . .

NCD: (*Cutting him off, pulling out a massive book, turning pages*) You mean someone like this?

Junior Creative: (*In tears of joy*) Yes, Sir!

NCD: So, let me just recap *my* idea for you.

(Junior Creative looks puzzled.)

NCD: There's a big Mercedes parked outside a stylish Edwardian villa with one of those Greek balconies with an iron railing, alongside a beautiful canal with a brilliant sunset in the background and a really hot girl and a hot dude. It's a picturesque setting with a line something to the effect of 'Gets your Attention', right?

Junior Creative: But it was my idea, Sir.

NCD: (*With an expectant nod*) Who came up with the Mercedes?

Junior Creative: You.

NCD: And the villa? And the Greek balcony with the iron railing?

Junior Creative: You, Sir.

NCD: The woman, the hot dude?

Junior: (*Gulps*) You . . .

NCD: The sunset? The canal? The location?

Junior Creative: You.

NCD: (*Sitting back in his chair, smiling*) Well . . .

Junior Creative walks out while the NCD makes calls to his photographer and travel agent for tickets to Venice for his latest idea.

The Junior Creative works till late at night as the NCD walks out, passes him, set to fly with *his* idea. Before he leaves, he calls the Creative Director to inform him about his plans, entrusting him with the upcoming Campaigns for the week.

All in a day's work in the life of the NCD.

Here's a test to see if you can some day become the NCD of a big Agency.

1. You are walking by your junior's desk and see some good Ads lying scattered over it. You:
   a. Continue walking.
   b. Congratulate the kid on his good work.
   c. Wait for the kid to go to the loo and sneak away with the prints.

2. A junior questions your idea at a meeting. You:
   a. Continue talking like you didn't hear a thing.
   b. Hear his argument out, congratulating him for his insight at the end of it.
   c. Sack him.

3. You are writing a script. It opens on:
   a. Your cabin; why go anywhere when you can do it here?
   b. A beach in Goa.
   c. A place represented by a small dot on the world map, still inhabited by Stone Age tribes.

4. Your cabin needs some renovation. You:
   a. Adjust yourself to sit somewhere else in the office.
   b. Work out of home till the cabin is ready for occupancy.
   c. Go on an *official* trip to an exotic location.

5. Your Agency doesn't win any award for a year. You:
   a. Inspire everyone to work harder.
   b. Hire more Creative people.
   c. Make sure *you* are on the jury of the next award show.

If you've answered all 'C', you have the makings of an NCD.

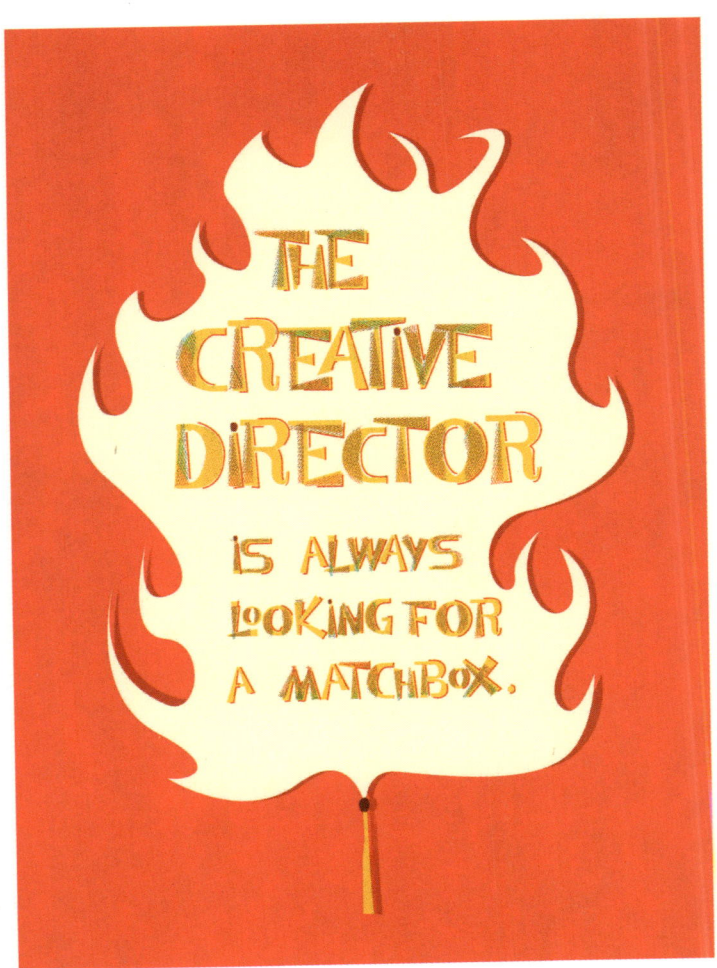

THE CREATIVE DIRECTOR IS ALWAYS LOOKING FOR A MATCHBOX.

The Creative Director, as the name suggests, directs Creativity (sometimes, along a one-way street from his juniors' computers into his portfolio). The Creative Director heads a group in an Ad-Agency, usually with teams of Creative under him. He's the one who is under the NCD and above the others. Everything that's reported to him, he reports to the NCD—including answers to important questions like 'What's for lunch?' The CD approves the work done by his team before it can be shown to the Client, or, if it's an important Ad, to the NCD. A painful process in which the Junior Creative wait for hours together for the Creative Director to finish with his meeting, usually being held in the closest bar.

There are two types of CDs—the Art CD and the Copy CD. They work as a team while heading a team at the same time.

The Copy CD is of the suave, well-dressed (changes his underwear once a week), smooth-talking variety. Remember the guy in college who'd get any girl he wanted? He's him, on crack. The Art CD is the one who's constantly surrounded by printouts of rough Ads, untouched food and trainees who always want approvals on their designs. The Art CD is the over-worked, over-paid, under-respected, taken-for-granted, always-insulted, ever-reliable, work-dispensing machine, a nocturnal insomniac who blames it all on his profession.

Becoming a Copy CD isn't easy. You need to have:

1. Spent at least a decade in one or more Agency (or have opened one yourself).
2. Enough unpublished long copy Ads that, when strung together, can become a book of at least 1,000 pages.
3. Examples of good writing—a collection of unknown writers' bodies of work which you can copy from and call your own.
4. Mastery over the art of procrastination.
5. The ability to make procrastination look like work.

But apart from these salient qualities, it's really easy to spot a Copy CD—crumpled jeans and T-shirt, flip-flops and messy hair—in Advertising that is 'well-dressed'.

'So what?' you ask. 'Isn't everyone dressed like that?'

Yes. But there's one differentiator—if you're sitting in the reception area of an Agency and someone matching the above description walks in around lunch time, you can safely assume that he's the Copy CD. ANYONE coming before lunch matching that description is probably a college student whom the Copy CD called in at 9.30 am sharp. Of course, the CD didn't make it because he worked really late.

It's really easy to tell an Art CD in an Agency—he's usually the one with any of these stock-images sites flashing on his monitor:

1. Getty Images.
2. Index Stock.
3. Corbis.

In case he doesn't have any of these on his monitor, he won't be at his desk; he'll be the one going around the office asking people a standard question: 'Do you know any good image sites?'

Apart from identifying these unmissable qualities there's a surefire way, too, of spotting an Art CD. Crumpled jeans, crumpled shirt, facial hair, and chappals. 'So what?' you say. 'You said the same thing about the Copy CD.'

Yes. But there is still one differentiator. While the Copy CD walks *in* after lunch, the Art CD usually walks *out* after lunch—having worked all night—and walks in an hour later again, wearing the same clothes.

Becoming an Art CD isn't any less difficult. You need to have:

1. Spent at least a decade or more in one or more Ad Agencies.
2. A sufficient number of Ads that, when neatly stacked, can act as a coffee table, but still somehow fit on your desk when scattered.
3. A good command over design (the ability to change your trainee's design, which he/she makes in two days, in less than five minutes).
4. A thorough understanding of your craft: having design books which only you own because only you can afford them.
5. A good network of people: friendship with the best freelancers in the industry.

Here's what an average day in the life of a Creative Director looks like:

3 am: Come home.

5 am: Go to sleep.

Noon: Enter office. Order tea/coffee. Check mails, decipher handwriting on post-its, chuck them into the bin.

12.15 pm: Listen to issues, ideas, excuses for needing a half day, free credit card offers.

12.20 pm: Walk around enquiring about lunch. Challenge someone to a game of cricket.

1.00 pm-2.00 pm: LUNCH! The most important part of the day. Eat off everyone else's plate. Order lunch. Get junior to eat it.

2.00 pm: Attend meetings. Check mails, Facebook, feel sleepy.

2.20 pm: Pretend to stay awake.

3.00 pm: Start thinking.

3.05 pm: Back to cricket.

4.00 pm: Coffee.

5.15 pm: Listen to trainees' complaints and ideas. Make jokes.

6.00 pm: Pick nose.

6.05 pm: Reschedule meetings.

7.00 pm: Start work. Think about the to-do list.

7.15 pm: Share bad jokes with the canteen guy.

7.30 pm: Get back to thinking.

9.00 pm: Go to the closest bar with a great idea.

9.05 pm: Pick nose.

9.10 pm: Idea doesn't seem great. Re-write brand name on a piece of tissue paper and start thinking again.

11.00 pm: Return to office.

11.15 pm: Play video games.

1.30 am: Feel good about being in Advertising.

2.30 am: Write a post-it for tomorrow. Shut down.

(The difference between a Copy CD's and an Art CD's day is the Art CD is always looking for images or new image sites and he doesn't go home.)

But it's not easy being a Creative Director either. Here's a test to see if you can be one.

1. Your junior tells you a great award-winning idea. You:
   - Continue playing games on your fancy Macintosh, completely ignoring him.
   - Pat his back and walk him into the NCD's room.
   - Tell him it has been done before and then present it as your own to the NCD.

2. Your trainee is feeling low and disillusioned. You:
   - Give him a pep talk.
   - Take him out for a drink to explain life to him.
   - Blame him for being too cynical too early.

3. Your junior seeks to get his work approved. You:
   - Walk to his desk or ask him to come to yours, immediately.
   - Continue playing cricket in the corridor.
   - Berate him for interrupting too much.

4. Some junior in your team suggests a new, expensive but useful book on design. You:
   - Call the librarian immediately and ask him/her to buy it.
   - Nod absent-mindedly and later accuse the junior of not taking permission before buying it.
   - Accuse the junior of having 'fancy demands'.

5. You have a meeting with the NCD early next morning. You:
   - Set an alarm to make it on time.
   - Keep pushing the meeting back, hoping to quit before it happens.

- Take the NCD out for a drink and, at 3.30 am, suggest delaying it.

However, the Big Bosses aren't good enough on their own. A Pitch also means pulling out Advertising's most potent weapon—the Brainstorm.

The Brainstorm is a gentle breeze of the A.C.

Brainstorming, a term commonly used in any Agency, is defined as 'shared problem-solving' in which all members of a group spontaneously contribute ideas, trying to solve a problem by rapidly generating a variety of possible solutions. Here's an example:

Let's buy Milds.

Gold Flake is better.

Do you have money?

I think I'm getting a divorce.

It's settled, *bidis* then . . .

It's really easy because the most important point about Brainstorming is that there's no pressure to be brilliant, which makes it more like a general meeting of people who all claim to be working for the same Agency but have never met. Once everybody's settled in, important topics are discussed: traffic snarls, bad chairs, worse salaries and worst canteen food.

Q. What is a Brainstorm?
A. Check the title of the chapter.

Q. Why is a Brainstorm held?
A. We need to Brainstorm to answer that one.

Q. How often is a Brainstorm held?
A. More often than required.

Q. What is usually discussed?

A. Latest movies, women in the office, low salaries, 'Where to go for lunch?' and lastly, 'Why are we here?'

Q. What is the ideal duration of a Brainstorm?

A. Till the pizza is demolished.

Brainstorming venues are chosen according to the people who call for them and the issues at hand.

Important Brainstorm:

These are usually held in an absurdly cold, Big Conference Room housing a table with the surface area of Goa, and comfortable chairs into which you can flop and forget the reason you came there. This sort of Brainstorm is when the biggest brains in the office come together to discuss a really important problem—like where they can have lunch. The Big Conference Room is the only place in the Agency, apart from the NCD's office, which has comfortable chairs. The rest of the Agency—and any Agency—has uncomfortable chairs, often with one broken castor, arm rests that look like they've been chewed, and back rests that go to and forth like a punching bag. (In spite of all this, chairs are found missing every morning, possible reasons for which are also briefly discussed during the Brainstorm).

Useless Brainstorm:

This is the sort when the marketing side of the business calls for a Brainstorm, usually held in the Small Conference Room of an Agency. This is the only Brainstorm which any Creative in his/her right mind or even in a drunken state, thinks is below him/her to attend. It's usually called to solve very minor problems like an invite for a party, a birthday card for the boss, an important presentation, etc. A sample useless Brainstorm goes thus:

Servicing: We need to Brainstorm.

Creative: Why?

Servicing: We need to come up with an idea for an invite for a party.

Creative: Not we, *you* need to come up with it.

Servicing: Oh, come on, I am sure it'll be fun.

Creative: It's below me to Brainstorm with you.

Ego hurt, Servicing decides to go it alone and, failing to come up with any ideas on their own, call for this sort of Brainstorm. Creative usually doesn't attend this kind of a Brainstorm citing important reasons like, 'I need to feed my cat' or 'I need to use the loo.' The few who do attend (they are called Trainees) come up with some basic ideas that are enough to excite Servicing.

Creative: What is the invite for?

Servicing: It's for this Client who has given us the maximum revenue for the year.

Creative stares at the ceiling or the table with an inward gaze. 'Okay, how about we have a currency note?'

Creative 2: With a line like 'Enough work, let's party.'

Servicing is excited. This is the point when Creative exits the room.

Unsure Brainstorm:

This is called for by Junior Creative. Usually held on the staircase of the building, this is a Brainstorm for the smaller problems—like designing a leaflet, or when the temperature of the AC drops too much, or when someone decides to use the Junior's chair as a stump for a game of cricket. Not completely aware of the golden rule of 'Not having to come up with ideas' in a Brainstorm, the Junior Creative try really hard, thinking it imperative to come up with them; backed by the fear of being called 'Un-Creative'. They are the only ones in an Agency who take a Brainstorm very seriously, but miss the whole point of a Brainstorm: the discussion of ideas. There is dead silence with everyone carefully scribbling something in their pads, not wanting to share their ideas because of the stories of stolen ideas they've heard when they were outsiders.

Creative 1: What are we here for?
Creative 2: I don't know. They said to come to the Small Conference Room.
Creative 3: So nobody knows?
Creative 4: Let's leave, then.
Unanimous: Okay!

Lastly,
Q. Does Brainstorming help?
A. Can we get to the next chapter now?

The NCD and CDs being given the responsibility of the Pitch assemble in the Big Conference Room on a day finally decided upon after many delays. The delays, of course, are caused by the hectic lifestyles of the CDs and because the NCD has to keep his cell switched off in airplanes and cannot be reached.

Scene: The Conference Room of a big Ad-Agency. The NCD gets up, takes a deep breath and speaks.
NCD: All right, boys (*bear in mind these are grey-haired, balding, pot-bellied men, the exact same people who call their trainees 'young men'*). We are pitching for a new business, a retail giant, Highstyle. The question is, what can we, as highly paid individuals, do about it? Any ideas?

There is a long pause (of approximately two days) with everybody thinking hard, staring at the table or looking out of the window. Finally, a hand goes up.

NCD: Yes . . .
CD 3: I have one.
NCD: One what?
CD 3: Idea.
NCD: Oh, it slipped my mind. What is it?
CD 3: What's what?
NCD: You said you had an idea.
CD 3: Ah, yes, that. Let's change it.
NCD: Change what? The topic?
CD 1: You mean the one we're discussing?
CD 3: No. The product and everything about it . . .
NCD: (*With a thoughtful look*) So, if I understand correctly, you think we should change everything about this brand, one of the most successful ones in the recent history of the retail sector, with a fierce following and loyalty?

CD 3: Yes.
NCD: I love it!

Proud nods of approval all around the table and the room is slowly filled with murmurs of 'Lunch, anyone?' And, 'Was I supposed to be here?'

NCD: It's settled then. Boys, it was wonderful Brainstorming with you. But I just realised that we can't really start without Planning; send them in immediately.
CD 1: So, what was this?
NCD: (*Winks*) Let's just call it a warm-up, shall we?

As they all leave, the NCD evaluates his progress—'official' trips, a nose job, the sacking of seven employees and this Brainstorm. So far, so good. Lost in self-admiration, he waits for Planning to arrive.

PLANNING

DOESN'T

HAVE

A PLAN   UP ITS

SLEEVE.

The Account Planner is that member of the Agency's team who is the expert, through background, training, experience and attitude, at working with information and getting it used—not just marketing research but all the information available to help solve a Client's Advertising problems. Yes, and China is the world's largest democracy.

Planners are a special species since they are so important to the process of making an Ad. Without a Planner, Ads wouldn't exist; neither would the chances of having free beer because there wouldn't be any long meetings to attend if they didn't make big presentations. The Planner is required for doing research on the brand, its competitors in the market, to convince the client that the Creative Ad isn't made on whims and fancies and when the ideas seem to be failing, to blind the client with numbers and stats, bar-graphs and market research. It's basically talking to the client in his own language, using jargon which usually sends most Creative into a coma.

Planning requires some special qualifications:
1. Readiness to wear formals to work (in an Agency, that's counted as a qualification).
2. A penchant for organising and attending meetings.
3. Convincing everyone about the need to attend meetings.
4. Googling everything.
5. Making long, endless presentations.

6. And making each slide look different.
7. Looking busy, while idling.
8. Having a thorough knowledge of affordable hotels that deliver food, all night, anywhere, in the city.
9. Being able to look intently at the monitor, straining to read something, but actually thinking about whom to borrow the next cigarette from.
10. Lastly, an understanding of products and consumer psychology (ha-ha).

The Planner and the Process:

Planning starts by studying the brief and doing research (usually on a thesis titled *Dodos, Our Real Ancestors*).

Then they prepare the brief—the piece of paper that the Creative subsequently plays 'Name-Place-Animal-Thing' on. The Planner briefs Creative. Interested Creative discuss women, why *their* bosses—or all bosses—suck, the latest movies, low salaries and nasal hair. The rest progress to Name-Place-Animal-Thing.

Once the Creative present the Ads—another free-flowing discussion of the things that matter—rising petrol prices, low salaries, making farting sounds with the lips, and more Name-Place-Animal-Thing. The Planner pre-tests the Ads, harassing a set of consumers—the only set that shares the lab-mice's pain—to check if they get it or not.

Once the Ads are out and the Creative is on their 'well-deserved' break, the Planner evaluates the campaign for effectiveness. (Again, the long process of surfing porn, looking for dateable women, exchanging important emails, exploring

the
planner

the *Playboy* Calendar Archives and doing further crucial research on the dodo paper.)

How good a Planner you are depends upon the size of your presentation—the number of slides being in direct proportion to the expertise of the Planner—anything around 100 being merely basic. It also depends upon how many meetings you attend and how distraught you look at any given point of the day.

Essential Facts about Planning:

1. There is a process for Account Planning.
(Eat. Drink. Attend meeting. Make slides. Attend more meetings. Eat. Drink. Burp. Fart.)

2. Account Planning is the key to winning the new-business Pitch.
(When Creative fails, gobsmack the Clients with numbers.)

3. Good account Planners are hard to find.
(They don't work in your agency.)

So, in comes Planning, to meet their new NCD, who is adjusting the crotch of his trousers. After a melee over chairs they settle down, ready to push their kidneys and the brain cells to their limits.

NCD: Gentlemen, we need to change a retail brand, completely, right from its name. I met with my boys but we all agreed that it is really up to you guys in Planning to help us out, to show us a way forward. The question is, how are we, highly-paid professionals, going to do it?

After many blank looks, a hand goes up . . .

NCD: Yes . . .
Planner 1: Let's break all barriers, by rising above the clutter of the category.
NCD: (*Gurgling with excitement*) Sounds great! How?
Planner 1: We'll analyse consumer patterns in the last year, dig out numbers on the shopping trends, identify the biggest shopping influencers of the past decade, interview prospective consumers, and observe the changing pattern of shopping over the years.
NCD: (*Takes a deep breath*) Anyone else?
Planner 2: Recycle the old presentation we used for the last Pitch . . . and change it completely, with a whole new opening slide . . .
(*A round of loud applause*)
Planner 3: But we lost the last Pitch.
NCD: Why did we lose the last one?
Planner 1: Which one was the last one?
Planner 2: Was it *Evita*?
Planner 3: That's Madonna's song. You're always on YouTube.

NCD: Actually, it's the MD's wife's name.

Planner 1: It was the strategy.

As everyone continues arguing, the NCD interrupts.

NCD: No gentlemen, it was the environment.

Planner: What do you mean?

NCD: You won't understand now.

Planner: You don't like the colour of the office?

NCD: It's not that. Nevertheless, let's get to work. And while you put the presentation and research together, send in Servicing, they have an important role to play here.

Confused, Planning leaves the room wondering what it could be that Servicing had an important role to play in.

Within an hour's time, in comes Servicing.

SERVICING
IS ALWAYS
AT
EVERYONE'S
SERVICE.

Before one understands what Servicing is and does, it's important to know how they got their name. When the government banned servitude, it posed a serious problem for the advertising industry. Not one to take it lying down, it decided to combine its most effective tools to solve problems: Brainstorm + Offsite. And considering the gravity of the situation, it flew a hundred miles to be one with nature, in Jaipur Palace.

Again, the NCD got up to speak.

NCD: We have a problem . . .
CD 1: Yes, the staff looks gay . . .
CD 2: Isn't the Palace supposed to have dancers?
CD 3: What are we here for?

After much debate, a heavy lunch and an afternoon siesta the team noticed a group (Servicing) on their way out.

NCD: Oh boys, we forgot! They still need a name.
CD 1: What has the law banned?
CD 2: Them in general.
CD 3: Look! Two of the waiters are kissing . . .
NCD: (*Gravely*) Don't worry, gentlemen, it'll all stay the same, we just need a fancier name to replace Slavery, like (*looking skyward*) 'Servicing' . . .
Nods and murmurs of 'I like it', and 'Let's go.'

And thus the Offsite had given birth to another gem: Servicing.

A Servicing job is really easy; qualifying for a Servicing job is even easier.

Things you need:

1. To be a glutton for punishment.
2. To have a thick skin.
3. An inborn and complete absence of self-respect.
4. A fondness for failure and rejection.
5. Fluency in understanding and speaking English.

Of course, the last one is the only one that's flexible.

Things you can do without:

1. Talent.
2. Personality.
3. A central nervous system.

Servicing is the de-facto peon, the link between Creative and the Client—which only means both turn to Servicing when they're having a bad day. Clients view them as menials and always think that they should've been ready with everything yesterday. This is based on a Visual Imparity Syndrome the Client suffers from: seeing Servicing as a delivery boy, at his beck and call 24 X 7, the absence of a tip being the only difference. On the other hand, the Creative think it below them to even talk to Servicing since they think Servicing is always wrong, because, well, they are . . . Servicing. According to them, they don't need any other reason. Servicing, on the other hand, think they're smarter than Creative because at least they have a real degree.

Scene: Late night. Creative sitting at his machine, working on an Ad.

Servicing enters.

Servicing: I saw the Ad.

Creative: Should we burn the CD?

Servicing: No, let's burn the Ad.

Creative: Don't try to be funny. You are Servicing.

Servicing: Okay, there's a problem.

Creative: (*Disgusted, opening the file*).

Servicing: The logo should be at the top.

Creative: No, it can't be.

Servicing: But it's a new show! We need to build the show; it has to be on the top.

Creative: Says who?

Servicing: Says my MBA sense.

Creative: Well, my design sense says it cannot.

Servicing: Why?

Creative: It just cannot.

Servicing: (*Grabbing mouse*) At least try.

Creative: (*Snatching mouse back*) If you take the logo up, we'll have to put the headline down.

Servicing: But it's the headline.

Creative: So?

Servicing: IT HAS TO BE AT THE TOP!

Creative: Says who?

Servicing: Show me even one Ad with the headline at the bottom. It's the HEAD-line (*grabbing Creative's neck, shaking it hard*). The head is always on top.

Creative: That's not true.

Servicing: And what about the colour?

Creative: What about it? You said it should be prominent and readable. And black is the most dominant colour.

Servicing: But, it's going to be dark.

Creative: What do you mean?

Servicing: It's a poster that's going to be inside a club. It's going to be dark.

Creative: So, who's going to tell me that?

Servicing: You're supposed to ask me that.

Creative: Since when? It's your job. You're supposed to tell me.

Servicing: Sorry, it slipped my mind.

Creative: How can it SLIP YOUR MIND?

Servicing: I'm saying, you're supposed to come and ask me if it slipped my mind. I can't tell you EVERYTHING.

At this point Creative leaves the argument and starts talking to the desk or the wall, hoping for greater intelligence.

The root cause of this mutual hatred is the nature of their work. Creative thinks Servicing makes senseless briefs because they don't understand what the Client says. The Client thinks the Creative fails because Servicing can't understand the Client and mistakes a brief for a piece of garment that covers a private body part.

The Client, a giant mall, needs an Ad announcing a sale. According to the Client and Servicing, this is a fairly easy, straightforward proposition. According to Creative, it's 'too' easy and lacks any interest value.

Servicing: Make a simple Ad announcing a 'SALE', up to 50 per cent.

Creative: What's the use? Even the Client can think of that himself. Why is he hiring us?

Servicing: To play cricket?

Creative: Shut up. Meet me in the evening. We'll figure out an interesting way to do this.

Servicing: Not 'we', 'you'.

Creative: Yes, I forgot. You can't contribute.

Servicing walks away. Creative, after a lot of thought, puts in an army tank with a woman standing beside it.

Servicing: (*Looking at it*) Are you sure this is a 'SALE' Ad?

Creative: Of course. The woman is going there armed.

Servicing: It doesn't work. Nobody will get it.

Creative: How can you say that?

Servicing: I didn't get it.

Creative: I don't see how Servicing can be the yardstick for society.

Servicing: The Client won't like it for sure.

Creative: It's such cynicism that's killing this business.

Servicing: Even if the Client approves this, how will we execute it?

Creative: That's your problem. You wanted an idea, I gave you an idea.

Servicing: I'm sorry. The Ad doesn't work. It's not according to the Brief.

Creative: Brief?

Servicing: I can't present this.

Creative: Why are you so afraid of the Client? He's supposed to take what we give him. He comes to us because he doesn't know better.

Servicing: I need an option.

Creative: I need a better Brief.

Servicing: It's a Sale Ad. How much simpler can I make it?

Creative: And that's the creative solution—a woman going there with an army tank to ward off others from the bargain sales.

Servicing: I'm confused between whether I should like it or dislike it.

Creative: So, what should I do?

Servicing: Give me an option.

Only one thing's certain: Servicing loses the argument because Creative walks out as soon as he's satisfied he's made his point, although the only sorry option he's offered is a gigantic board displaying the word 'SALE' in bold, virulent lettering. So Servicing goes to the Client with an Ad and one option.

Client: I wanted a Sale Ad.

Servicing: Yes, Sir, it *is* a Sale Ad.

Client: So what's the army tank doing there? There's no war in my MALL.

Servicing: It's a Creative solution—a woman going there with a tank to prevent anyone else from getting there.

Blank looks.

Client: Show me the other option.

Servicing: *(Hesitantly)* Here.

Client *(Jubilantly)*: Great! Can we make the logo bigger?

Servicing: *Wants to say, 'Personally, I don't care about your logo or what you do with it. The truth is, a bigger logo doesn't make a difference. You think by increasing the logo by 2 mm it will REALLY make a big difference? Do you think anyone even notices your logo? Or cares about it? I personally think talking to you is a waste of time. Goodbye.'*

But he says: Yes sir. I shall get it done.

Servicing comes back and tells Creative that the good Ad's bounced. Creative blames Servicing for not having the ability to sell it.

First humiliation

Servicing's boss is involved. Based on a career full of humiliation, he makes a few in-depth remarks . . .

Servicing Boss: Hmm . . . So, you couldn't sell it. Just make the logo a little bigger and this will fly.

(*Proud nods of approval.*)

The Ad is remade and goes into a second round.

Servicing: (*Carrying the same Ad with a bigger logo*) Sir, we believe in this Ad.

Client: Hmm . . . Okay. I hate the font of the headline, can we change the font? And cut down the copy too?

Servicing: (*Rushing back to office*) The Ad got bounced because the Client doesn't like the font.

Creative: Do you even know what a font is?

Servicing: Can you even spell 'font'?

The Ad goes into a third round and now the boss is involved. And so is Creative's boss.

And because the deadline has been missed in this chaos, so is the Client's boss.

Servicing boss's boss: (*To his subordinate who's Servicing's boss*) Hmmm . . . you couldn't sell it. Just make the logo a little bigger and make the background a little brighter.

(*Proud nods of approval.*)

But after the first two rounds of failure Creative decides to present the Ad along with Servicing.

Client: I don't like it.

Servicing: Why?

Client: I don't know. I just don't.

Servicing: Can you be more specific?

Client: No.

On their way back, Creative, who has been dead silent in the meeting, blames Servicing and his lack of conviction for the Ad's failure.

Servicing: You made this Ad. You should carry more conviction. You were sitting silent there. Why didn't you say something?

Creative: That's not my job.

Servicing: So, why did you come?

Creative: I just wanted to see how bad you were.

Third humiliation

The Ad goes into a fourth round. This time, the CSD (Client Servicing Director) is involved.

CSD (*Looking at Ad*): Hmmm . . . you couldn't sell it. Just make the logo bigger, the background brighter and highlight the main message in the copy.

(*Proud nods of approval.*)

They all go together to the Client's office; he rejects it again, this time on personal grounds.

CSD: You should've tried to sell it.

Servicing: But you were doing that, Sir.

CSD: At least you could've said something.

Servicing: What could I say?

Creative: You MBAs are absolutely useless. How can the Client say the colour doesn't work? Does he or do you even understand colours?

Servicing: So, why you telling me all this like it's my fault?

Creative: Everything is always your fault.

Fourth humiliation

Since Creative has bombed four times, the Client's boss calls up the VP.

The VP calls in the CSD, the CD and Servicing.

Scene: The VP's cabin. The VP looks at the Ad and takes a deep breath.

Everyone begins by blaming Servicing.

VP: You can't sell an Ad.

CSD: Or close taxi doors.

CD: You're an MBA.

VP: What was the problem?

Servicing: Creative.

VP: What exactly was it about Creative?

Servicing: Colour.

VP: Are you being racist?

Servicing: No, Sir, by Creative I meant the Ad, not the person.

VP: (*Looking at the Ad*) I think the Ad works. It's just that you couldn't sell it. Just increase the size of the logo, make the background a little brighter, change the headline, highlight the offer in the body copy and most importantly, change the visual to something like (*pointing to a* Playboy *cover*) this. I'll come for the meeting this time.

Servicing: The Client wants to see an option.

VP: So?

CD: I don't think we need an option. We need someone with selling skills.

Servicing: The Client asked for an option.

The VP tells the CD to try another option while they all take a pledge to call Servicing a prostitute. The CD agrees and tells his juniors to think of something while he goes to the closest bar. The VP goes home.

Servicing sits waiting.

Creative bounces off a rough idea at 8 pm for Servicing to start preparing his resources to make an artwork. Servicing goes to the Studio Manager to beg and plead for a resource.

Studio Manager: This is not the time; you need to make a booking.

Servicing: But the deadline is tomorrow.

Studio Manager: I don't care, you need to make a booking; I can't spare anyone right now.

Servicing: Should I talk to someone?

Studio Manager: You already are.

Servicing: Isn't it at all possible?

Studio Manager: (*Angrily*) No.

Servicing: But Creative gave the layout this late.

Studio Manager: That's not my problem.

Servicing: The Client is being unreasonable.

Studio Manager: That's not my problem either.

Servicing: Please?

Studio Manager: NO.

Desperate, Servicing makes a few calls. His boss calls the Studio Manager. The Studio Manager refuses to bend.

Studio Manager: Servicing's boss is still Servicing.

Frantic, Servicing makes a few more calls. This time, the CD calls the Studio Manager. The Studio Manager immediately agrees.

Fifth humiliation

There's a dummy required too. So now Servicing pleads with the Production Guy—Babloo or Raju—to stay back too, and who also throws a fit.

Servicing: Please, I need a dummy.

Dummy guy: By when?

Servicing: Late night.

Dummy guy: No.

Servicing: The Client is sitting on my head.

Dummy guy: How is that my problem?

Servicing: I'll give you free cigarettes all week.

Dummy guy: You said that last week too.

Servicing: This time, I will.

Dummy guy: You borrow mine every day.

Servicing: I know.

Dummy guy: How do you live with yourself?

Servicing: It's not easy.

Dummy guy: (*Sighing pityingly*) Okay, I'll wait.

Sixth humiliation

Finally, the idea comes at 11 pm.
The design starts after midnight.
The dummy's ready by 4 am.
A quick shower and shave later, Servicing is back in office, to show them what he's made of, but since the VP is coming for the meeting, Servicing is reduced to carrying laptops and parking cars.

Seventh humiliation

Scene: Big Conference room. VP, CSD, Servicing and the Client sitting in a round-table conference. The Client is a classmate of the VP from their B-school days.
The VP merely places the Ad on the table.
Client: Let's go with it!

Eighth humiliation

Servicing comes back to office and bumps into Creative.
Creative: You can't even sell one Ad.
Servicing: I still think the Ad didn't work but the Client can't wait any longer.
Creative: You don't understand Creative.
Servicing: You don't understand English.
Creative: You are *Servicing*.
At which point Servicing stops arguing, fully aware that he doesn't have anything worse to say to the Creative after that epithet.

Ninth humiliation

It's not even lunchtime yet.
Finally, the Ad is ready for release but the Client hasn't sent an estimate. Since Servicing can't go ahead without a signed estimate, he asks the Client to send one.
Servicing: I need an estimate.
Client: So what can I do?
Servicing: Can you make one and send it across?
Client: How dare you?
Servicing: Right, I'll fax you one. Just sign it and send it back.
Servicing makes an estimate himself and runs to the fax machine begging the Fax Guy to fax it.
Fax Guy: Do you even know my name?
Servicing: Now is not the time.
Fax Guy: Say my name or fax it yourself.
Servicing: (*Actually thinking*) The Fax Guy?
Now the Fax Guy throws a fit (based on the same premises as the Studio Manager, the Production Guy, the Creative, the Client, the VP, the Janitor, and the VP's pet dog Bossy).

Tenth humiliation

Servicing calls the Client and begs him to stay on to sign the Estimate and send it back.

Client: Why can't you ever do things on time? What part of 'yesterday' do you not understand? Why can't you be responsible? Why am I paying you? Send it immediately; I'm waiting. If it doesn't come in the next five minutes, your boss will have to sack you. That's a promise.

Eleventh humiliation

The estimate in place, Servicing begs the Studio Manager to do the final artwork. Studio Manager throws another fit because of the last-minute request.

Twelfth humiliation

Finally, work starts at 11 pm.

Time for the next problem—prints. Servicing now begs and pleads with the Printer.

Printer: Why can't you do things on time, man? Each and every time, why should my boys wait? This is not the first time. But this will be the last time. Just because *you* don't have a life, doesn't mean *we* don't have a life. Now hurry, we're waiting.

Thirteenth humiliation

As if this is not enough, the Media Guy calls to inform that the deadline's been missed. So this time, Servicing begs and pleads with the Media Guy to push the deadline and stay back in office since the artwork's almost done. The Media Guy throws a fit too (yes, still the same premise—nobody needs or has a stronger reason).

Fourteenth humiliation

It's 2 am, and since there's nobody to dispatch the Ad, Servicing takes it himself to the printing press and, this time, the Printer throws a fit.

Fifteenth humiliation

Finally, the Ad goes into printing and Servicing comes back to send the Outdoor Ads to other cities. Servicing begs and pleads with the Cargo Guy, who throws a tantrum of his own, to hold the cargo for some time.

Servicing: (*Running to reception*) I need to send a dispatch for cargo.

Watchman: Nobody's in the office, Sir.

Servicing: So who can go?

Watchman gives a blank look.

Servicing: (*Sighing*) All right.

Servicing carries the final printouts himself and manages to deposit the cargo just in time.

Sixteenth humiliation

And Servicing comes back to do the whole thing again with some other brand.

Another day in the life of Servicing.

Servicing comes to know they've been called into the room and they start preparing for the meeting—tucking in their shirts, sponging coffee stains off their trousers and telling the Canteen Guy to arrange for some more coffee; already feeling a strange sense of excitement within. This is the first time someone important has called them for something important.

Scene: Servicing enters. The NCD is dozing on the conference room table.
Servicing: You called a meeting, Sir?
NCD: (*Opening his eyes with an effort*) Yes, it's important.
Servicing: Are we getting better chairs?
NCD: No, no such luck. We're pitching for a retail giant. The question is, what can I, as a highly-paid individual, and you, as poorly-paid professionals, do about it?
Servicing: We do whatever you or anyone else asks us to. That's our job.
NCD: Well, Planning is doing all the research; you can try and help them. Take printouts, make sure the coffee's hot; the ink in the printer doesn't run out—you know, that sort of thing. (Nods of understanding.)
NCD: By the way, why did we lose the last Pitch?
Servicing: We are all new, Sir. We weren't there.
(Everyone's always new in any Agency.)
NCD: You guys weren't here and we still managed to lose the Pitch? Surprising. Do you think this office environment is conducive to thinking great thoughts?
Servicing: We wouldn't know, Sir.

NCD: Right, I should've known. But I think it was the right kind of environment that was lacking.

(Nods of agreement.)

NCD: (*To nobody in particular*) I am glad you agree too. It's settled then. We're all set for the Offsite!

(*A loud round of applause.*)

NCD: Well, why don't you guys take care of the Offsite?

Servicing: (*Collectively*) Can we make the presentation?

The NCD: No, that would be like giving a monkey the controls of a 747.

Servicing: So, what do we do?

NCD: You (*pointing at one*) . . . Take care of the drinks.

Three exit enthusiastically.

NCD: (*Pointing to a second*) You, decide on the menu.

A few more scamper out of the room as others look on expectantly . . .

NCD: You, inform everyone in office with a mail.

Two jump to it.

NCD: (*Pointing at nobody in particular*) You, decide the venue.

(They all exit the room in a hurry.)

The NCD stands smiling, admiring everyone's enthusiasm and his own vision.

Yes. It was time for the OFFSITE!

the offsite is not worth it?

Creative are known to think anywhere. That becomes their best excuse to look lost all the time, prompting taunts— like 'You creative types!'—from cousins, aunties, uncles, grandparents, parents and everyone else. They think in bathrooms, while watching TV and even while having sex. Some common tricks Creative perform to come up with ideas:

a) Playing Tic Tac Toe.
b) Browsing through *Award Annuals*.
c) Travelling.

Some common places in which Creative try to come up with ideas:

a) Coffee shops.
b) Bars.
c) Gardens.

This is the reason Advertising professionals say they're working all the time. To the untrained eye, it may seem like they're studying the pattern of the grass, but they're actually coming up with ideas for Ads or Campaigns for products of grave importance, like safety pins. But after the first few minutes, it just comes down to making inane observations about everything, which, to an inexpert eye, seems useless, but actually they're collecting situations and instances which they can use at some time in their Advertising career. And it's when all these times, tricks and places fail, that they have to use their trump card: the Offsite.

The Offsite is a gathering of all 'important' Agency-ites in a ridiculously expensive place to Brainstorm, hoping the venue inspires originality of thought.

Here are a few things you need to have to qualify as important:

1. Grey hair or acute baldness.
2. You need to be mature enough—maturity being judged by age; age being judged by a person who remembers how it was before Google.
3. An ego you are completely unaware of.
4. At least five pieces of work which you call *only* yours— since they were completed while travelling on official trips.

Once inside the big ballroom with a rent of Rs 1,00,000 (yes, per minute), the session starts with, not wanting to appear self-congratulatory, a *few* rounds of beer.

Many cigarettes later, as the day progresses, lulled by the cigarettes and the absurdly low temperature of the AC, everyone visits the toilet at least fourteen times, in between rounds and rounds of discussion about the bad location, the food, and the design of the carpet.

NCD: I hope slide 862 made things very clear, boys.
CD 1: Is it lunchtime yet?
CD 2: Can I quit?
CD 3: What was the presentation about?
CD 1: I feel I've seen it before.
Planner: Of course you have! It's the presentation we used the last time. But did you notice the new bright background?

NCD: Boys, any bright ideas yet?

CD 1: Yes, lunch.

CD 2: Let's just concentrate on the brands we already have.

CD 3: Or how about we take a quick recap of the presentation?

NCD: Good idea! I have one too.

CD 1: What?

NCD: As you saw in slide 643, there was an interesting insight into how the product has changed society.

CD 1: Let's cut to the chase.

NCD: So, how about we show the evolution of society with the product? Right from the Neanderthal man?

CD 2: Brilliant idea. I have one more.

NCD: Yes, go on.

CD 2: How about we go home?

NCD: But the beer isn't over yet!

Once the gossip, slides, pizzas and beer are emptied, so is the Offsite.

Immediately after their meeting with the NCD, Servicing sends in mail informing all the important people about the Offsite and, their joy knowing no bounds, everyone sets out in the middle of the afternoon to celebrate the occasion.

Next morning, as Planning makes its presentation, Creative (volunteers of 'Counting the Planning Head's Hairs Programme, a brainchild of the last living brain cell running on one gallon of beer since the previous afternoon) looks like it's jotting down things. After 127 slides and the counting of 3,210 strands of hair, there is an extravagant lunch, with starters, soups, every cuisine to suit the individual tastes of all the seniors, followed by a heavy dessert or two. Victims of the heavy meal, everyone spends the afternoon studying shoe laces, doodling, playing dumb charades, counting the number of people in the room wearing glasses and feeling good about being in Advertising.

After a few hours of mind-numbing discussion about the presentation, there are some pressing questions on everyone's mind:

1. Why did the presentation have a naked picture of Paris Hilton or was it an illusion caused by the girl who made the presentation?
2. What exactly is Retail, does it involve a lizard growing a second tail?
3. Was Planning making personal stabs by constantly saying 'Highstyle'?

The NCD finally gets up to speak.

NCD: Gentlemen, it was wonderful to have learnt of so many insights into the category and to see Paris Hilton nude on a large screen.

CD 1: The dal was too cold.

CD 2: Anything for the Gulab Jamun-Eating Competition Winner?

NCD: There was a competition like that? Nobody told me!

CD 3: We're ready.

NCD: (*Proudly*) That's the spirit, guys. Let's bring sparkling ideas to the floor.

CD 3: To leave, we meant.

NCD: So, any routes?

Planning Head: Let's give Creative what they always want.

NCD: What?

Planner 1: Considerate deadlines?

Planner 2: Beer.

CD 1: Let's go home.

CD 2: Is this the same Offsite?

NCD: I like the idea of giving Creative what they want. But what?

Planning Head: Complete creative freedom. No Brief!

NCD: Oh yes! Creative freedom! Boys, the Brief is, there's no Brief. Do what you want. It's a winning strategy.

CD 1: I need more beer.

CD 3: Can I scribble in my resignation?

NCD: (*Gurgling with excitement*) Look at this as the opportunity of a lifetime. At this crucial juncture, I would like to show you some Ads that have helped me to reach the top. (*As the NCD plays Ads dating to a time when the deadliest disease was the common cold, most lapse into a forced coma.*)

The slide-show over, the NCD continues to speak.

NCD: I hope that was inspiration enough to create work that's fresh and barrier-breaking. Get your teams together, let's see Campaigns next Tuesday. Good luck, boys. Remember the Brief: there is no Brief!

Brief is the proposition which contains the one thing the Client claims his product does that nobody else's can. That's why it's called the USP (Unique Selling Proposition). The Brief is made by Servicing and Planning—Planning doing most of the thinking, Servicing taking care of the printouts.

The Brief is the basis on which Creative comes up with ideas. Without a Brief, Creative is a bunch of guys playing cricket in the middle of the afternoon, only, in mufti. It's the only thing that prevents Creative from playing cricket all day long; since it gives them the luxury of an option when they're tired— conducting a spelling bee among themselves.

The Brief, sent in by the junior person at the Client's office, basically says this:

1. *Problem*: I am desperate. My boss has come up with an idea that lacks any merit but now wants some good Ads to somehow mask that and sell (*insert name of product or service to be sold*).

2. *The Proposition*: What the product or service does, which is the one thing that separates the product from the 247 others already in the category. But, if the others can make you fairer in seven days, this will do it by the sixth afternoon. If it fails, you can call the company for a full refund (that's why the telephone number and the fake email address are tucked in at

the bottom of the Ad and in a size so small that if some over-zealous fellow did read it, there'd be no way to establish contact—though it's difficult to tell since nobody's ever tried).

3. TG: (*TG stands for Target Group or the people for whom the Ad is primarily made. E.g. sanitary napkins' TG is women and shaving cream ads are directed towards men, simple.*) This is how an Advertising Brief describes a person: SEC AB or SEC A+ or any letter after SEC. (SEC: Suspiciously Evolving Cartoons.) It's widely believed that defining a person as SEC (Socio-Economic Class is what it actually stands for) takes care of it all. According to the Brief they do exist in a broad, abstract sense. Just like the government's common misconception that installing street lights will automatically make streets safer and lower the incidence of crime. He or she doesn't need a name; age is anything between fifteen and thirty-four (somehow, *every* Brief is targeted at youth); nobody knows what they like or do. The TG is the one most likely to ignore the ad, eating bhel-puri in it or sometimes even making rockets with it in class, where there's at least hope that the professor will pick it up and read it to the class, when again it will be ignored by more than half present, which is already half of the TG—so, to catch them at places they are most likely to catch it are also included. (If you thought the last line was confusing, wait till you read a Brief.)

4. The Media: Radio spots they can turn off, hoardings they can drive past, newspaper Ads their parents can

read, standees in malls to be seen while they're busy calculating complex equations between CP (Cost Price) and BP (Budget Price), television Ads, so that they know when to change channels.

5. The Budget: The most important and often absent word in the entire Brief. It's usually the point when Creative starts playing mind games with the first person he meets.

6. The Deadline: Falls usually on a day before the date on which Creative gets the Brief.

Any Brief travels a lot en route the brain of Creative.

Getting Briefed:
This is the part when the Client Briefs Servicing. It involves a high-level meeting at which Servicing is usually given a stool to sit on in the huge Conference Room as the Client explains what his product is, the proposition, how much he expects to achieve by Advertising for it.

Client: So, that's the product and all its attributes. Are we clear?

Servicing: Yes, Sir.

Client: Good. I am looking to launch this product in the market like it has never been done before—with hard-working, honest Ads. I want them to elaborately explain all the attributes of my product, have a nice big logo, make it bright and colourful so that it stands out in dull newspapers. I am looking to achieve results and impossible sales targets with this. Don't worry about the money. Are we clear?

Servicing: I'll go back and brief Creative immediately. When is your deadline, Sir?

Client: It was yesterday. Let's see some Ads.

Servicing rushes back to office and immediately (in approximately ten hours) convenes a meeting with Creative.

Briefing:

This is the second destination in the journey of the Brief; where Servicing Briefs Creative.

Servicing: Guys, this is a new product. The Client wants to launch it in a big way.

Creative: Where's the pizza?

Servicing: The Client wants to spend a lot, so budgets are not a problem either.

Creative: They all start by saying that. If money's not a problem, where's the beer and pizza?

Servicing: It's supposed to release in a few weeks. The Client wants to see the first cut Ads by the end of the week.

Creative: Which Client is this?

Creative 1: Which meeting is this?

Servicing: Perfect, I'll mail you the Brief.

Servicing mails Creative a Brief outlining everything he had managed to write down in the meeting. After a couple of days, Servicing meets Creative who are playing cricket with a paper ball.

Servicing: Guys, are you working on the Brief?

Creative, completely ignoring the question, hits the paper ball right into Servicing's hand.

Servicing: Hey, this is my Brief!

Creative: Yes, we were just going to get on to it.

The Brief continues to travel as the Creative, too busy with something, nobody knows for sure what, decide to Brief their Trainees.

Re-Briefing:

Creative: There's a new product.

Trainee: (*Excitement-filled eyes*)

Creative: It's all clearly written down. Come up with a few ideas and let's sit sometime at the end of day.

The Trainee grabs the Brief thinking it to be the biggest opportunity of his life while Creative walks away hoping to find another Brief to make a ball with.

At the end of the day, the Trainee waits impatiently for his seniors to come back—from where he doesn't really know—armed with a bundle of ideas, all of which he thinks are winners. With Creative nowhere in sight, the Trainee calls them.

Trainee: Hello, ya, hi! I'm (*he gives his name*).

Creative: No, I don't want any credit cards.

Trainee: But I'm not selling credit cards. I'm the new Trainee. I am waiting to discuss ideas for the Brief you gave me in the morning.

Creative: Oh . . .

Trainee: I was wondering when we can sit?

Creative: Tomorrow. Remind me. I have left for the day. But think a little more till then, anyway.

Trainee: Oh.

The next morning, Creative enter at around lunchtime to find the Trainee waiting impatiently for them.

Trainee: I have some ideas.

Creative: Not now, man, I have to leave for a meeting.

Trainee: But Servicing has asked me for them ten times since the morning.

Creative: Ask him to fuck off.

Trainee: Can *I* say that?

Creative: It's Servicing. Anyone can.

Trainee: So, when can we sit?

Creative: As soon as I come back from the meeting. But keep thinking.

Finally, after a couple of days, Servicing catches up with Creative.

Servicing: Did you crack that Brief?

Creative: No, man. Give me half an hour.

Creative searches frantically for his Trainee, who is out for lunch with his college friends, boasting of his cool job which gives him the privilege of asking his seniors to fuck off.

Creative: Where are you?

Trainee: I am out for lunch.

Creative: And who is going to discuss those ideas? It's been three days. Come back to the office right now, let's sit on the ideas.

The Trainee rushes back to the office and has his ideas shot down within minutes.

Creative: What's the use of hiring you?! Go call Servicing.

Servicing enters, hope scrolling in his eyes.

Servicing: All right, let's hear the ideas.

Creative: We don't have any, man. Give us till the end of day.

Servicing: All right, but you're clear on the Brief, right?

Creative: No, actually. It'd be great if you could just run me through it again.

Thus, the Brief travels again.

At the end of the day, Servicing looks frantically everywhere for Creative.

(*Entering library enthusiastically*): Guys, hope you're on the Brief already?

Creative: (*Showing him the Brief*) Ya, man, can you tell me where I should put my next 'X'? He's put an '0' here. (*Pointing to the mark.*)

The Creative don't think on the Brief immediately; they always let it 'sink in', hoping it will do the 'sinking in' by itself just by being carried around. After a week of Briefing, Servicing finds it on the footpath and waves it in the face of Creative.

Servicing:(*Angry*) What is this?

Creative: Oh, that's the Brief I was looking for!

Servicing: I found it on the street.

Creative: Ah! I was letting it sink in for a bit.

Servicing: Do you have any ideas? The Client is after my guts.

Creative: You can't expect us to perform like this, man. We're not machines. Good Ads need time.

Servicing: You've already taken a week.

Creative: Yours is not the only Brief, you know.

Servicing: I understand, but at least . . .

Creative: Shut up, man. Besides, it's not even clear.

Servicing: You want to be Briefed again?

Creative: That'd be great.

Thus, the Brief travels full circle; completing its journey over a couple of pizzas before finally sinking into the cluttered desk of the Art Director.

The Brief doesn't ever sink. Campaigns do.

The Creative Director, having completely forgotten to Brief his team, calls a meeting late at night.

CD: (*Calling his Copywriter*) Hello . . .
Copywriter: It's 11.30.
CD: (*Urgently*) We have a meeting. Come to the office right now!
Copywriter: Hello?
CD: (*Angrily*) It's urgent, where are you?
Copywriter: (*Sleepily*) In the library. Is there a Brief?
CD: Maybe!

The Creative Director, happy to know that the Copywriter's around, calls his partner, the Art Director.

CD: (*On the phone*) Hello, where are you?
Art Director: Hello?
CD: Come to the office right now . . .
Art Director: Hello?
CD: All right, I see you; you're at your desk . . .
Art Director: No, seriously, hello?

Pulling the Copywriter out of the library, they convene at the desk of the Art Director, who's busy working.

CD: Boys, there's a Brief . . .
Art Director and Copywriter listen intently . . .
CD: It's a *nice* Brief . . .
Art Director and Copywriter are slightly confused.
CD: Ya, as I was saying, there's a nice Brief.
Art Director and Copywriter: (*Growing restless*) What?
CD: It's about freedom.
Copywriter: (*Quickly jotting down a line*) Yippee! A social service Ad for 15th August.

CD: No, no, I mean, the Brief is that there's no Brief. Do what you want . . .

Art Director and Copywriter: (*Together*) You mean *anything*?

CD: Yes. Just, for Highstlye.

The Team: (*Together*) *Any*thing?

CD: Yes, anything. That's the Brief. No rules, no mandates, go for it . . . This might make or break your careers . . .

(*Blank looks.*)

CD: So, when can we sit on the first round of ideas?

(*Blank looks.*)

CD: Thursday it is, then!

The copywriter is always out for lunch.

The Copywriter is the most important person in an Agency, or at least that is what his actions suggest: eating a huge breakfast, sleeping after lunch, playing football in the hall, ordering in expensive snacks, quaffing endless cups of coffee and, of course, working late because he didn't do any work during the day. In any Agency, these are the things one would commonly find on a Copywriter's desk:

1. A stolen pen.
2. Lined pages torn out of a child's exercise book.
3. Grass, not the environment-friendly sort.
4. A cheap replica of the Taj Mahal (or any other wonder of the world) embedded with a small clock that doesn't work.
5. A sex toy.
6. Other battery-operated toys: an abusive parrot, a crawling soldier and a vibrator that comes in handy (no pun intended).
7. A tiffin box with rotting food dating back to the day he joined.
8. A stack of *MAD* magazines.
9. A snap of his baby nephew.
10. A ready letter of resignation conspicuously placed—'just in case'.

The Copywriter gets away with all of this is because they're all somehow work-related. He's allowed them because his is the most difficult job: industriously scribbling a line or two on the back of a movie ticket before stepping importantly out to lunch. Ask anyone in any Agency—that takes some doing.

Coming up with a line is not as easy as it looks; the Copywriter needs:

1. To play Hangman or any other such word-game—using the Law of Averages to complete any given row—for at least three hours to get going.
2. To eat all the food in the office and since it wasn't enough, to step out for lunch again.
3. Sound sleep, preferably on office furniture, during the day.

On an average day, the Copywriter juggles at least six to seven Briefs (one being the fresh one, the others, leftovers from the previous night when he was 'working' hard). Dedicating time for each leaves little or no time for other work; which just piles up as more work for the next day. And so on and so forth. And that's why the Copywriter's the busiest on any given day.

The biggest challenge a Copywriter faces—apart from finding a decent place to sleep—is unwanted advice from everyone, since they think English is the only qualification required to be a Copywriter. They can't argue with the NCD because he can never be contacted, nor the CD because nobody knows what a CD does (including the CD), nor Servicing because everyone has too much self-respect to approach them. Another problem is that every Client has once aspired to be a writer, or still yearns to be one deep down inside him and sees every Brief as a chance to fulfil the dream.

Scene: The Copywriter, who's just completed writing a Brochure, discussing it with the Client over a conference-call.

Client: I like it overall, I am not happy with the Introduction.

Copywriter: (*Straining to hear*) Oh, okay, what about it?

Client: It doesn't sound believable; I am searching for the truth.

Copywriter: Have you tried Googling it?

Client: I feel the first line is too long.

Copywriter: On which page? (*Scrabbling to find the paragraph being discussed.*)

Client: Hello?

Copywriter: Yes, the first line of which page?

Client: Aren't we discussing the Introduction?

Copywriter: We were, but you said some first line. So are we okay with the first line?

Client: No, it's the first line of the Introduction.

Copywriter: What about it?

Client: It's too long.

Copywriter: The Introduction?

Client: No, the first line. Can you cut down that line from fourteen words to, say . . . (*Thinks purposefully*) around five words.

Copywriter: But that's not possible; I only have verbs, nouns and basic infinitives in the line currently.

Client: But it's too long.

Copywriter: There's nothing fancy; it's a factual line, it has all the things YOU said you wanted in the Introduction.

Client: I know all that, just cut it down to five words.

Copywriter: How?

Client: That's where you come in.

Disconnects.

The Copywriter goes back to writing it all over again, and the making of a Brochure goes on for at least six months.

Another tricky part is proof-checking an Ad or a Brochure or a Leaflet or the CD's second cousin's nephew's wedding card. (The proof-checker leaves at 6 pm and a Copywriter typically checks the Ad only after that, being busy with more important things like getting a date and checking his armpits for anti-date odour.) While the others sign the Proof—which comes in only after 1 am—at a glance, the Copywriter has to read each and every word, even the address line tucked away at the bottom. This takes a considerable amount of time, most often longer than the time taken to write the Ad in the first place. Given how busy the Copywriter always is, he overlooks a spelling mistake (popularly known as a 'typo'). And the only person who spots it is the Client (because he is the only one who bothers to read the Ad), who gets angry, takes it as a personal insult and takes it out on the CD. The CD's ego hurt, he seizes the opportunity to vent all his frustration—his failing love affair, his receding hair line, and the growing amount of money owed to the cigarette stall—on the pretext of the copywriter's typo.

CD: There's a typo in the Ad.

Copywriter: You actually read it?

CD: You are supposed to know the spelling of endeavour . . .

Copywriter: I do.

CD: So why is there a typo? Didn't you spell-check?

Copywriter: Microsoft Word didn't point it out.

CD: Microsoft Word? That's your benchmark?

Copywriter: But you asked me to use the Word spell-check.

CD: Yes, but I didn't think you'd use it. Do you know how much that Ad cost us?

Copywriter: (*Nobly*) I'll pay for it from my own pocket.

CD: You can't. With your salary, it'll take a century, and the government has banned bonded labour.

Copywriter: See? I told you I was being given too low a salary. What do we do about it, then?

CD: The Client's pissed. Let's make a nice mailer to score brownie points with the Client.

Copywriter: How about we tell the Client that nobody except he will read that line?

CD: Write that mailer by the end of the day.

Copywriter: But it's 1 am.

CD walks away.

The Copywriter doesn't work as a stand-alone; he needs as a partner someone he can blame at the end of the day. And the unfortunate person playing that part is the Art Director.

THE ART DIRECTOR: FIRST, SKIPS LUNCH, AND NEVER GOES HOME. THEN SKIPS DINNER

The Art Director is the most overworked, underpaid person in the entire organisation and yet gets little respect—because everyone thinks he can only recite A to Z in roughly three hours and two minutes. The Art Director ideally has, or is supposed to have, basic knowledge of design, colour and typography. These requirements are the very things that everyone—yes, even the receptionist—questions, criticises and makes conclusions about. And the very people who hire the Art Director because they don't know anything about Art, are the first ones to sit back and point out 'mistakes' with regret in their eyes.

Scene: Art Director, tired and puffy-eyed, calls the CD to come see the Layout before it can be sent to the Client.
Boss: Ya, give me a minute.
The longest minute recorded in the history of mankind begins before the CD is done with more important activities—lunching, smoking and playing pocket billiards. Finally, tired of waiting, the Art Director is on his way out—when the CD catches him.
CD: Hmmm . . . I like it (*long pause*), but . . .

A crowd assembles behind them—Servicing, the Copywriters, and the other teams.
CD: (*Drawing a deep breath*) Maybe the background colour could be brighter. What do you think, guys? (*The original group has disappeared; there's a new group now. The new*

group includes the canteen guy waiting to be paid for the day's uneaten food, and the receptionist who's come to tell them that the Art Director's father has sent a message.)

Canteen guy: Total Rs 47.

Receptionist: I think it's an emergency. He's called many times.

The Art Director obediently grabs the cursor, dragging it in senseless glee till the CD asks him to stop.

CD: You think the font colour works?

Receptionist: (*Hurrying in*) He just called again. That makes it forty-eight times.

Canteen guy: (*Seizing the opportunity*) Yes, forty-eight! For now, the font colour changes.

CD: I don't like the headline. Where's the writer?

Art Director: But you had approved the line yesterday.

CD: I don't like it today. Where's the writer?

A wild-goose chase ensues for the writer, to finally find him asleep in the library. The writer, looking offended, walks in and re-writes the line, but mistakenly on his jeans, as he's still half-asleep, and walks off.

CD: Let's replace the line.

Art Director: But, he's not given the line.

CD: Of course, he wrote it.

Art Director: He didn't give it to me.

Receptionist: (*Panic-stricken*) Make it fifty.

Canteen guy: (*With greed-crazed eyes*) Yes! YES! Fifty!

Another chase starts for the Copywriter who prefers to send back a small piece of his jeans. The Art Director types it in and starts playing with the mouse again.

CD: Great. But is this is the best image we have?

Art Director: (*Frantically opening folder of references*) No, I had many more.

CD: (*Getting up to leave*) Well, let's see three or four different Ads with better images. This one doesn't work. You need to be able to search good images.

And that's Art Direction in a nutshell—picking the right images off the Net and placing a line given on a piece of paper (this time on a rag of denim) under it.

Next morning, the Copywriter comes out of the library looking as fresh as a daisy and eager to see the Ad. The Art Director is dozing off.

Copywriter: How can you sleep, man? There's work to be done.

The Art Director gets up and shows him the entire folder.

Copywriter: (*After looking at 17,194 images in the folder*) I don't think they work. None of them is eye-catching.

Art Director pulls out a blade from his drawer.

The Copywriter opens a new site very quickly; types in a new 'keyword'; picks up a new image.

Copywriter: This is good.

Art Director: (*Dropping the blade*) Okay.

The CD walks in a few hours later and comes immediately to the desk.

CD: Let's see.

Art Director shows him the Ad.

CD: (*To Copywriter*) Great! I'm sure you chose the image.

Copywriter nods in acknowledgement. They walk away for a smoke.

Art Director walks to the canteen to get a knife.

Once the Ad is made and approved, Servicing goes and presents it to the Client, and comes back with it looking like the Art Director's English answer-sheet in school, because Servicing doesn't open his mouth to defend the Ad (maybe out of spite, because Servicing isn't fond of the Art Director), and is used to acting like a clockwork dummy. On the rare occasion that the Art Director gets to meet the Client, they strike up a friendship on the common ground of hatred for Servicing. The Art Director takes in all the changes himself and both sides experience the first pure communication in their lives. Overwhelmed, they sign an agreement on the closest square of tissue paper; making it The Official Document of Mutual Respect and Understanding (ODMRU), agreeing to eliminate Servicing completely. The Art Director makes his own brief and with new-found hope and respect for the profession, churns out options at will.

But come the time for presentation, the Client with whom the ODMRU was signed is out of town (the tissue paper is already decomposing and recycling itself into a new plant). Left with no option, the presentation is made to the Junior Marketing who was rudely excluded from the ODMRU.

And it falls flat again.

After rounds and rounds (repeat till bored) of approvals and rejections, an approval makes its way to the Art Director's inbox, much to his jubilation.

It's finally time for the actual shoot.

The Art Director shortlists Photographers and asks them for quotes, without telling them what they're shooting.

Art Director: Hello, yeah hi, I'm calling from an Agency. There is a Campaign to be shot. I wanted an estimate.

Photographer: Okay. What's the campaign about?

Art Director: It's for a bank.

Photographer: What's the media plan? Print or hoardings?

Art Director: That's not decided yet.

Photographer: Approximately when will the shoot take place?

Art Director: I'm not too sure.

Photographer: Roughly how many shots?

Art Director: I can't pinpoint a number yet.

Photographer: What is the budget?

Art Director: Not too much.

Photographer: So, then?

Art Director: Send me a quote, that's all.

Photographer: I need details to quote a price.

Art Director: I need a quote first. Here's my email id. Mail me your quote.

Photographer: Can you mail me references, at least?

Art Director: Yes. But I don't know if those shots are final. So I don't know if that'll help.

Photographer: What do you know for sure?

Art Director: That I need a quote.

(*Line disconnects*) After trying a number of Photographers the Art Director gets three quotes and goes to the CD for his approval.

Art Director: I have three quotes from three Photographers here.

CD: Each?

Art Director: No. One from each.

CD: Who are they?

Art Director names the first one. The CD shoots it down for personal reasons. (The photographer has a grander house than his.)
The Art Director gives the second name.
The CD rejects it for professional reasons. (The Photographer mistook him for the tea-boy in the last shoot, which they did exactly a zillion years ago.)

The third one is rejected 'generally'.

CD: How about a foreign Photographer? I have one.
Art Director: Have you seen his work?
CD: No.
Art Director: Does he have a site?
CD: I'm not too sure, but mostly, no.
Art Director: So, how can we be sure he's good?
CD: He's from Europe.
Art Director: That's a qualification?
CD: Of course, he's a foreign Photographer, he HAS to be good.
Art Director: You want me to call him to the office?
CD: No, don't bother. Let's go to him.

Art Director calls the Photographer.
Art Director: We need to meet.
Photographer: Yes.
Art Director: Can you come to the office?

Photographer: Hello?
Pause.
Photographer: Come to my Studio!

Art Director: Hello?

After a long discussion, they agree on a neutral venue like a coffee shop (now you know why advertising people are all in coffee shops, all the time).

If the Art Director is ambitious (low-salaried), they start on the same table but the Photographer leaves the conversation when the Art Director mentions the word budget because it's the amount the Photographer spends annually on underwear. The Art Director leaves with the bill. It's the recipient of the message which is received minutes after dispersing—*'Nice meeting you, looking forward to working with you'*—that decides the course of the entire shoot. If the Art Director gets the message, the Photographer comes to the Agency, agrees to the models chosen (even if one of them is his wife) and agrees to dates for the shoot too. If the Photographer gets the message, the shoot doesn't take place.

There is no such thing as a middle ground.

All this decided upon, it's time for the Recce.

The Recce is a pleasure trip of two or more days in a luxury car when the team goes out to a remote location to choose a spot for the shoot. It's an intensive research of different locations before they decide on the final location for the shoot. It's a painfully long process that consists of:

A HUGE breakfast.

A HEAVY lunch.

Drinks.

Snacks.

On the way, the car pulls up on a lonely highway to meet the Set Designer, who gets into the car, makes a few rough sketches on any surface he finds, including the car seat. The meeting lasts for not more than four minutes. Finally, they decide to shoot, but realise the light has faded and it's not enough to take even test shots. (That explains the two days.)

On the second day, the Art Director strikes wild poses at the location, fulfilling his/her ambition of being a model, to upload on popular sites for the world to seethe in envy of his job.

On the day of the main shoot, the Set isn't ready, the Stylist usually doesn't get the clothes asked for, the camera doesn't work, and the Client shows up too, having problems with everything: the location, the camera, the Photographer, the models, even the position of the sun. He chooses a new point, which is approximately 0.004 inches away from where the Art Director first decided.

Art Director: But, that's not a good place.

Client: I think it works.

Photographer: I think I see an anthill.

Female Model: I think I've slept with you (*looking at all three men*).

Male Model: (*Looking at Client*) Me too!

The shoot underway, the Client's complaints keep increasing

Client: I don't like the picture.

Art Director: What about it?

Client: Can we get a better model?

Art Director: It's just the angle of the laptop (*shifting it by 0.001 inch again*).

Client: Ya! That's a great shot!

Finally, the shoot is over and they all go—no, not home, that would be so un-advertising-like—to the first bar in sight while the Art Director goes back to office with the images on a DVD.

It's time for the Layout.

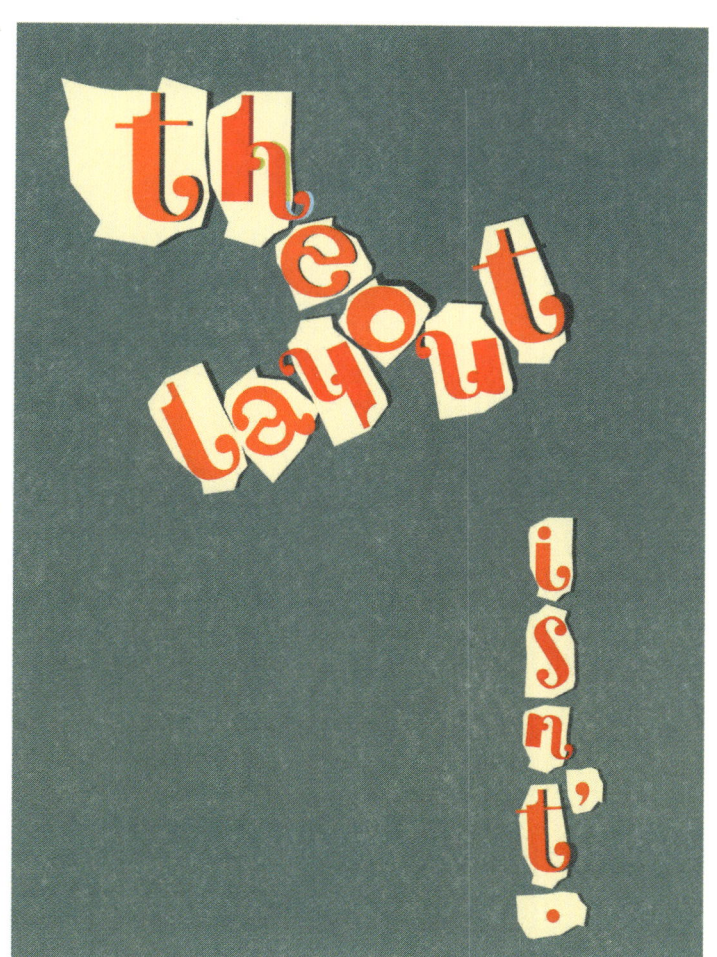

the layout isn't

The Layout is the arrangement of all the elements in an Ad—the logo panel, the logo panel, the logo panel, more logos, and only if needed, a visual and a headline—in an attractive way, so that it enhances eye movement. The biggest logo should be seen first and then, whatever else that may be on the Ad.

There are many types of Layouts depending upon the media, the time of the day or the week and, if the Art Director is a girl, the time of the month.

1. I-have-Lost-My-Mind-Layout (these are generally made after 1 am).
2. I-Hate-My-Job-Layout (Monday morning products).
3. Why-Am-I-Doing-This-Layout? (After the receptionist points out changes in your Layout).
4. Is-This-My-Life-Layout? (One done late on Friday evening).
5. My-Life-Sucks-Layout (One done on weekends).
6. I-Quit-Layout (One made in roughly 0.8 minutes inside the boss's cabin, with the words 'I QUIT' scrawled with a thick black sketch pen held in the non-writing hand.)

The Client, on the other hand, is worried about the money he's putting in. That's one reason the Client is seldom invited to the office—the fear that he'll have multiple heart attacks starting at the reception itself and finally giving way when he sees someone asleep in the library at 3 pm. And the only thing that can assure the Client that his money isn't being used only for lazy people sleeping all day or enthusiastic people playing football and table tennis, is the LAYOUT. And that's why the Layout is the most important thing to the Client; because it's the only proof that SOMETHING IS HAPPENING. (It doesn't matter if it looks like it sucks.)

Art Director: (*On the phone at 2 am*) Sorry, Sir, I hope I didn't disturb you.
Client: (*Slightly angry*) This had better be good.
Art Director: Sir, I mailed you some Layouts.
Client: (*With an excited shriek*) I am coming to the office right now. GIVE ME THE LAYOUTS!!
The Client's car skids out at night towards the office.

There is nothing that pleases a Client more than seeing a Layout—not his child taking his first steps, not a happy wife, no, not even a promotion. Some Clients go to the lengths of staying single just so that they can stay out late hours to SEE THE LAYOUT! The Layout Addiction Syndrome is something that assails every Client.
These are the sounds you can expect to hear in a Client's office:
'Can I see the Layout?'
'Can I see the Layout?'
'Can I see the Layout?'
'Can I see the Layout?'
'Can I see the Layout?'
'Can I see the Layout?'

'Can I see the Layout?'
'Can I see the Layout?'
'Can I see the Layout?'

Once the Layouts are done, the Proof is called for.

THE PROOF

Proves firsts, aproves later.

The Proof is a printout of the Ad on the actual paper of the media—newspaper, hoarding, etc. It is also the piece of paper also acting as a coffee table near the Art Director's desk. As the name suggests, it's the proof of what the Art Director was trying to tell his CD all through the process of making the Layout.

Art Director: Can I order Proofs?

Boss: Why do we need Proofs?

Art Director: We need a Proof.

Boss: A Proof or Proofs? Decide.

Art Director: No, I mean, we need a Proof, so we need the Proofs.

Boss: Have you read *Wren and Martin* yet?

Art Director: So, do I call for the Proofs?

Boss: No, my personal bungalow has eaten into the budget.

Art Director: So?

Boss: So, what are you here for? Why did I hire you? I thought you knew what colours look like. You said you could tell blue from light blue. You lied in the interview. (*Getting worked up.*) Did I make a mistake? (*Louder*) Tell me! Tell me I made a mistake.

Art Director: You're taking this personally now.

CD: (*Looking like a balloon ready to burst*) So, what do you want me to do?

Art Director: Call for Proofs, Sir.

CD walks away. Art Director calls for Proofs.

As with every Proof, the first round always goes wrong.

Art Director: (*Proofs in hand*) The colours look pale.

Boss: I like the logo.

Art Director: But, the colours look pale.

Boss: Well, that's your mistake, you chose them.

Art Director: What now?

Boss: Call for more Proofs.

Art Director: But the deadline was yesterday.

Boss: Doesn't matter, the Proofs are most important. Keep them coming.

The Art Director sits at his desk, calling the Printer who's sent in the Proofs.

Art Director: The colours look bad.

Proofs Guy: Hello?

Art Director: And, there's a copy error too.

Proofs Guy: Hello?

Art Director: Wait, the logo's wrong too. It's a different Ad!

The conversation ends in two ways, depending on the Art Director.

Ambitious (*low-salaried*) Art Director: Forget it, I'm coming to your office and getting prints done!

Settled (*high-salaried*) Art Director: It's cool. Let's go with it.

As the Proofs keep coming, the Ad undergoes changes.

Scene: The Art Director is looking at more Proofs. The CD passes by. Looks at the Ad.

CD: Is that a monsoon offer Ad?

Art Director: Yes.

CD: But we're in October.

Art Director: The first Proof came last December.

CD: And wasn't this the New Year Ad?

Art Director: Yes, but we missed the deadline.

Boss: Where's the writer?

The writer walks in looking tired. (All the pending work, remember?)

CD: You wrote this?

Copywriter: Yes.

CD: Change it.

Copywriter: But this is the Proof.

CD: I mean, change it to Diwali. (*Turning to the Art Director*) And you, put in a cracker or two.

Art Director: We'll need more Proofs.

CD: (*Walking away*) Don't worry, we still have Christmas.

Art Director: There's another problem . . .

CD: What?

Art Director: The crackers . . . I can't draw.

CD: But you went to Art School.

Art Director shrugs.

CD: So, now?

Art Director: I know a good illustrator.

CD: Okay, we have the money for this. Give it to a freelancer.

Freelancers are a special breed in the business. They're the talented lot who make more money than most employees' annual income, in a single assignment.

Being a Freelancer has its advantages:
- You wake up at a decent hour, 11 am.
- You don't need to travel during peak hours every day.
- Privacy. When you need to scratch, you don't have to settle for a hasty grope behind the copying machine, you can sit back, stretch your legs and go wild with a fork.
- You are your own boss.
- You are also the courier boy.
- Oh sorry, this was the list of advantages.
- Good money.
- But it never comes on time.
- Drat! Advantages only. Sorry.
- You can work in informal clothes—such as your jockeys.

This special breed is called upon to perform important tasks which the Art Director isn't expected to be able to do—drawing, for instance.

In spite of going to the same art school, the Freelancer makes probably a zillion times more money than his batch mate, the Art Director, who calls him.

Art Director: Hey, I need a favour.

Freelancer: I charge for favours too.

Art Director: Oh come on, we go back a long way. Do this in the friendship account.

Freelancer: (*Utters a bad word.*)

Art Director: Okay, do it for the least possible amount; I don't have much money for it.

Freelancer: What is the Brief?

Art Director explains the Brief.

Freelancer: What is the deadline?

Art Director: Yesterday.

Freelancer: Okay, I'll do it, but promise to see to my payment.

Art Director: I'll settle that, you start work.

Line disconnects.

The Art Director walks up to Servicing and tells him the Freelancer's quote.

Servicing: What? That's more than my annual salary.

Art Director: Yes, but there's a difference between you and him.

Servicing: It's more than YOUR annual salary.

Art Director: Look, you want this done? I've asked him to start work.

Servicing: See what you can do, man, this is too much.

Art Director: I'll see what I can do.

Empty promises on both sides made, the Art Director completely forgets about the matter and goes back to Googling for more image sites.

After a few hours, the Freelancer sends in some sketches and one is finally decided upon. The Freelancer has to send the final file but it's too heavy.

the
freelancers

Freelancer: I can't attach it.

Art Director: Can you come and drop it off?

Freelancer: Can't you send anyone?

Art Director: Okay, I'll see what I can do.

Art Director calls Servicing to his desk and explains the problem to him.

Servicing: So? We need to send someone?

Art Director: Yes.

Servicing: Why don't you go? You can catch up too; he's an old friend of yours.

Art Director: I don't even care if this Ad is released; you do. You go.

Servicing, without any real option, fetches the DVD from the Freelancer's place and in the meantime, the Freelancer mails the Art Director the bill, which the Art Director blindly forwards to Servicing.

Servicing: (*Holding the bill*) What is this?

Art Director: It's the Freelancer's bill.

Servicing: Yes, but you said you were going to do something.

Art Director: (*Snatching back the bill*) I will.

The Art Director calls the Freelancer.

Art Director: Dude, this is too much.

Freelancer: Bro, you said you'll make sure the amount's no problem.

Art Director: Yeah, man, but this is too much. It's more than the CSD's annual salary.

Freelancer: Who is he?

Art Director: Doesn't matter.

Freelancer: So why are you telling me? I don't know, man, I can't do anything.

Line disconnects.

Art Director: I spoke to him. He can't reduce it.
Servicing: What? He's only drawn some silly crackers. Even I can do that.
Art Director: But *he's* done it. Now get this bill out as soon as possible.

The Art Director takes the illustration to the CD, who approves it.
CD: Good.
Art Director: Sir, we'll need Proofs.
CD: Keep calling for Proofs. We have till Christmas.
Art Director: You mean to clear the Freelancer's bill?

And all that trouble later, final changes are made in the Studio.

The Studio has no Time Zone.

The Studio is the busiest, most efficient place in any Agency, with hard-working, simple men who are complete misfits in the business, working away meticulously, doing their thing, guided by a bored, lethargic or dead Art Director sitting behind them, 'directing' art. The Art Director makes a design. This design is used pan-media—in hoardings, press ads, leaflets, etc. But the Art Director thinks it below him to use the same design and make Ads of different sizes. Mindless work, it's called. And that's where the Studio Guy comes in. The Studio Guy uses different crops of this design and fits it into different sizes.

Art Director: Yes. Make the logo slightly bigger now.
(*Studio Guy stretches the logo to make it bigger.*)
Art Director: Now shift it to the right.
(*Studio Guy presses the arrow key.*)
Art Director: Stop! Now make it slightly smaller. Two per cent.
Studio Guy: (*Frowning*) Now?
Art Director: Yes. Now, save it. (*Ticking in his long list of sizes*) Delhi 20 by 30.
Studio Guy: But the file name here is Mumbai 20 by 30.
Art Director: (*Coming out of his coma*) Shit. This is the wrong file. Zoom out.
Art Director: (*Looking at the entire Layout*) Damn! This is the wrong logo. We have the wrong Client.

Studio Guy smirks.

As the Art Director leaves to smoke another cigarette, wondering what went wrong, not just in the Layout but in his life in general, another one comes and asks the Studio Guy to open another file for another Client for another Campaign.

Studio work never ends; with one adapt followed by the other, the Studio Guy works at any hour on any day of the year. There's no such thing as Saturday, Sunday, Monday. This is the basis on which anyone working in an Agency says, 'We're working all days of the week. There's no such thing as weekends or holidays.'

If all adapts in the list are done and the Campaign is out, they still have work ahead of them because the street outside the MD's house doesn't have any hoardings or kiosks.

MD: Is the Campaign out?

Art Director: (*Proudly*) Yes. It's all over the city.

MD: How come there's none outside my house?

Art Director: Sir, the media plan didn't include the street where you live, because yours is the only house there.

MD: So?

Art Director: So, we have hoardings where our TG is . . .

MD: So you think you can completely ignore me.

Art Director: (*Getting the drift, running to the Studio*) You know the Campaign we just wound up? Make another Ad in the size of a kiosk.

And the Studio Guy opens the file again.

Studio and Art Directors share three kinds of relationships:

1. *The Studio Guy and a Senior Art Director*: This relationship is based on awe and respect because they

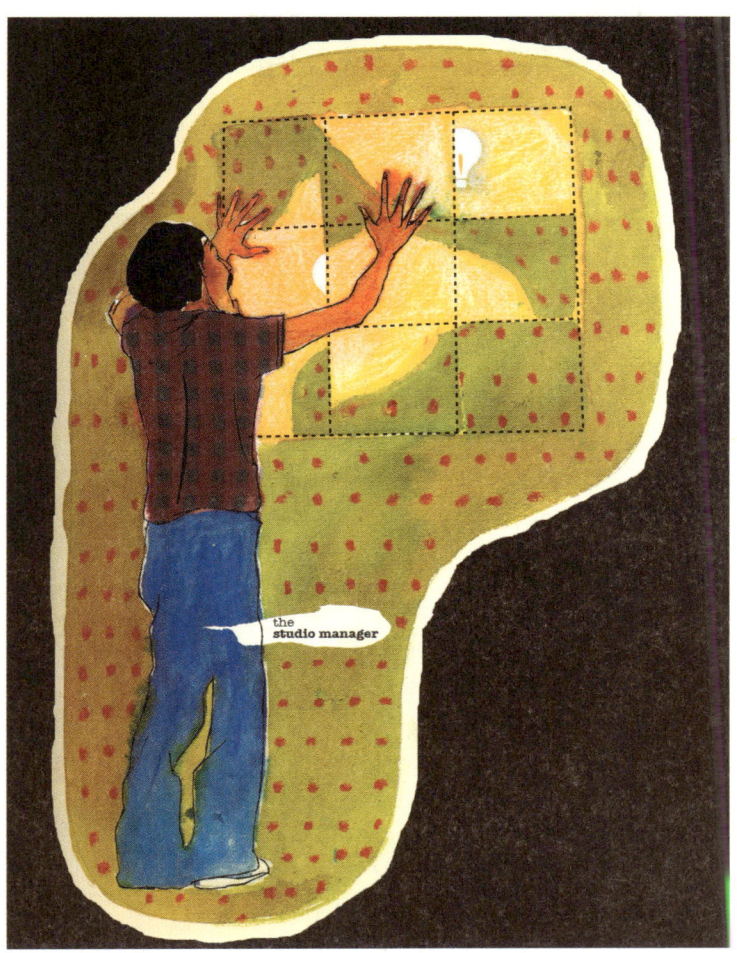

are often of the same age, and the Studio Guy, who puts in twice as many hours but walks away with an amount the Senior Art Director spends over lunch, wishes he were him.

2. *The Studio Guy and a Good Art Director*: A relationship that's based on mutual respect and affection because the Studio Guy wishes that he was what the Junior Art Director is at that given age.

3. *The Studio Guy and a Bad Art Director*: A relationship that consists of meaningless time-pass and silly jokes; a special kind of bond where the Studio Guy gets to call the shots in any Layout.

Art Director: Make the logo smaller.

Studio Guy: No, no. Let's keep it big.

Art Director: It's too big.

Studio Guy: But the size of the Ad is bigger too.

Art Director: (*A glint of enlightenment in his eyes*) Yes, of course.

Another special type of relationship the Studio Guy shares is with Servicing, who is the person usually sitting behind the Studio Guy getting all the adapts done, the long media list in hand, while the Art Director sits in the closest bar, happy to see the back of the Campaign. Servicing gives instructions that he has taken from the Art Director.

Studio Guy: Now what has to be done in this Ad?

Servicing: What do you mean?

Studio Guy: Are you sure this colour is fine?

Servicing: Which city is this for?

Studio Guy: This is for Delhi.

Servicing: Yes, the green is right. Or did he say red? Let me check.

Servicing calls the Art Director to clarify and it usually turns out that both—Servicing and the Studio Guy—are wrong.

Studio Guy: Now which logo has to be the biggest in this panel?

Servicing: This is Delhi, right? The Radio Partner logo.

Studio Guy: But last night Art Director Sir made the Radio Partner logo big in all Mumbai hoardings.

Servicing: Are you sure?

Studio Guy: No.

Servicing: Open the files, let's see.

Studio Guy: The files are too big. The computer will hang.

Servicing: (*Calling the Art Director*) Okay, let me check.

In the meantime, the Art Director has already downed three more pegs.

Servicing: Did you make the Radio Partner logo bigger in Mumbai hoardings?

Art Director: Hello?

Servicing: Hello, it's me. Which logo should be kept bigger in the Delhi hoardings?

Art Director: Sorry? Hello, I don't understand.

Servicing thinks it's the network and starts walking around the office.

Servicing: Is it clear now?

Art Director: What?

Servicing: My voice. Should we make the Radio Partner logo bigger in Delhi hoardings or the TV Partner's?

Art Director: Hello?

The line is disconnected.

The Studio Guy loses it because he has to open all the files again while Servicing heads out for a smoke.

Speed of Work Getting Done and the Kind Of Art Director are always inversely proportional. Once all the sizes of all the Ads for all the cities of the massive Campaign are done, the final printouts are taken—the all-important set called the Artwork.

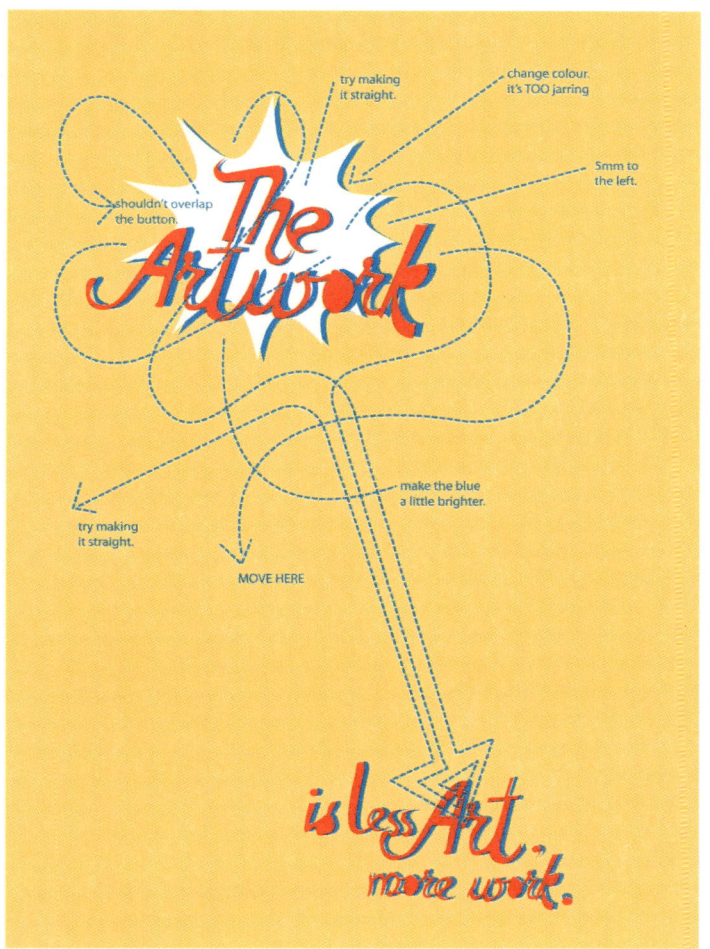

The Artwork is the final, final, final, okay-now-it's-really final, this-is-the-*finalest*-of-the-final, 'if-this-isn't-final-I'm-shooting-you' version of the Proof of the Layout, just before it goes to the printer to be blown up into huge sizes for homeless kids to build shelters with. No, sorry, for hoardings to distract you while driving, or print Ads for you to use to wrap stale food or an apple core.

The Artwork has a stamp area with space for signatures of the entire team—the Art Director, the Copywriter, Servicing, etc.— which means the Artwork roams around a diameter of approximately thirty miles of the office to be signed and sent back with oil stains, patches of sambar and—if it's coming back from the Copywriter—dried vomit. And sometimes, empty of signatures.

But the Ad doesn't go out before all of them have signed on it. (If the Copywriter has passed out before the final print comes out, thumbprints are okay, too.) The Artwork is compiled in a huge ugly book called a Guard Book which is the ultimate threat to Creative.

Servicing: There's a spelling mistake in the invite.

Copywriter: You have a cigarette?

Servicing: A big mistake.

Copywriter: Maybe. But who's signed it?

Servicing: You!

Copywriter: (*Evil laughter like the* Batman Comics' *villains*) That's what you think.

Servicing: (*Frantically turning pages*) Oh God!

Copywriter continues evil laughter.

Servicing: (*Ecstatic*) WAIT! There's dried vomit! I can prove this. I need your DNA sample.

Copywriter's laughter fading . . .

Servicing: Let's go to bed.

Copywriter: (*Snatching book*) Let's burn this first.

And after all the above, the Ad is finally released in the paper. A few years after the Art Director first thought of it.

The next morning, the Copywriter comes in with the newspaper.

Copywriter: I saw the Ad.

Art Director: (*Silence*)

Copywriter: The shoot looks really okay.

Art Director: (*Silence*)

Copywriter: The colours look slightly pale, man.

Art Director: (*Silence*)

Copywriter: The logo looks too big, too.

Art Director: (*Silence*)

Copywriter: The font of the headline is bad, it isn't even readable. But it's cool; do you have the model's phone number?

At which point the Art Director introduces him to a new Brief. And it starts all over again.

The Copywriter and Art Director, excited with the new Brief, of having no Brief, decide to Brainstorm to come up with first-rate ideas, first thing next morning.

10 am.
Art Director: Let's sit around 12.
Copywriter: Cool.

12 noon.
Art Director: Dude, you wanna sit now?
Copywriter: (*Busy playing Hangman*) No, man, got lots to finish. Let's sit post-lunch.

3 pm.
Art Director: Dude, you ready?
Copywriter: I said post-lunch man.
Art Director: It's 3 already.
Copywriter: (*Looking slightly cross*) Didn't I SAY the time is post-lunch? Tell you what, I'll come to you.

7 pm.
Copywriter: Dude, I'm ready. You wanna sit?
Art Director: (*Busy looking at Proofs*) Slightly tied up, man . . . Gimme half an hour.
Copywriter: (*Angrily*) Dude, you can't keep pushing it, mar; we'll never get to sit together if we carry on like this.

9 pm.
Art Director: (*With pad and pen in hand*) Dude, let's go.
Copywriter: Let me just grab a quick bite, man. Half an hour?
Art Director: Cool, I'll knock off some other things.

11 pm, the Copywriter comes back.

Copywriter: Cool, let's sit.

Art Director: (*Yawning*) I'm tired, man. Let's do this first thing tomorrow morning.

Victims of First-Thing-Tomorrow-Morning Syndrome, the Copywriter and Art Director finally sit to Brainstorm one late night.

Art Director: Cool . . . so what are we doing for this?

Copywriter: Can you show me the Brief?

Art Director: There isn't one.

Copywriter: We NEED a Brief, man.

Art Director: Let's make one.

Copywriter: Right (s*tarts rolling a joint*).

Art Director: I mean a Brief.

Copywriter: (*Starts hurrying*).

Art Director: It's for Highstyle, that's all we know.

Copywriter: You wanna have a take on the style of people?

Art Director: Sounds good, how?

Copywriter: That we'll figure out tomorrow, man.

Art Director: (*Getting up to leave*) Cool. First thing tomorrow morning then.

Copywriter: (*Sedated by the joint and the AC*) Yes, yes. First thing.

Next morning, the CD comes asking for the Ad.

CD: Guys, anything yet?

Art Director: Ya, we thought of having a take on people's style.

Copywriter smiles proudly.

CD: And what with it?

Art Director: We're figuring out.

Copywriter smiles more widely.

CD: Right! So, second half today?

Unanimously: Yes.

Post-lunch, they bump into each other outside the office, smoking cigarettes.

Art Director: You said let's sit second half.

CD: What?

Copywriter: On the Highstyle thing.

CD: What's the Brief?

Art Director and Copywriter: (*Confused*) There's no Brief.

CD: So what do you want to sit on?

Art Director and Copywriter together: The ideas and Ads.

CD: But you said there isn't any Brief. So how are there any ideas?

AD and CD together: But that's the Brief. And that's the idea.

CD: Stop wasting my time. Just show me some Layouts and we'll take it from there.

So, even more confused, the Art Director and Copywriter sit and crack some ideas while the Copywriter starts writing lines at the Art Director's desk and the Art Director looks for images.

A few hours later, the Layouts ready, the Art Director calls the Copywriter to see the Ads before they are formally presented.

Copywriter: The images don't look good, man.

Art Director: The lines are very average.

Copywriter: (*Opening a new site and typing in a new keyword*) There.

Art Director: (*Selecting the line and starting to type a new line*) There.

Copywriter: Cool. Works!

Art Director: Cool. Works!

And the wildgoose chase begins for their Creative Director, whom they finally find downstairs.

Art Director: (*Showing Layouts*) Here they are.

CD: (*Squinting*) The colours don't look right.

Art Director: That's because of the streetlights.

CD: Hmmm . . . You're right. The line isn't so good.

Copywriter: (*Spontaneously*) I think it's the streetlights.

CD: (*With a grave look*) You're probably right. (*Deep drag*) Good work, boys! Just add the logo and keep it ready. Let's present this First Thing Tomorrow Morning.

The Copywriter and Art Director work entire nights to make Campaigns, using every kind of Ad in the book.

The Radio Spot (Or Jingle):

The Radio Spot is also called the Radio Jingle if it is jingling; that is, if it is a musical, rap or a small song. The Radio Spot is one of those Ads which the Copywriter usually records on his own, without the Art Director. It's more of the Copywriter's baby, though sometimes the Art Director comes up with the idea and sometimes the script too. A Radio Spot requires a script which is approved word for word by the Client, which the Copywriter narrates over the phone or in a meeting. After the script is approved and almost re-written by the Client with changes in words and sometimes even spellings, a 'scratch' is made. A scratch is the rough Radio Spot, much like the reference that an Art Director uses before an actual shoot. The Copywriter chooses the best voice in the office or in some cases does it himself. This happens because the Copywriter always realises what is needed at the last minute, which is too late to persuade anyone else to leave their other important work—such as abbreviated pingpong across their desks.

Once the scratch is made, Servicing mails it to the Client.

Servicing: Sir, did you hear the spot?

Client: Yes, the voice isn't too clear.

Servicing: It's a scratch, Sir. We'll be using a professional VO (Voice-Over) artiste for the final spot.

Client: I don't like the background track either. It's too racy.

Servicing: Sir, but it's for the shopping festival.

Client: I know, but can it sound a *little* racy and not *too* racy? You know, right now it's like a sprint. Let it sound like a jog.

Servicing: Sir?

Client: Ya, right now it comes off as a kid running. It should sound more like a young adult with a slight paunch running. You know what I mean?

Servicing: (*Giving up*) Yes, Sir. I'll see you at the recording, Sir.

For the final recording everyone assembles in the Sound Studio at 11 am (or any other decided time)—the Voice-Over artiste, Servicing, the Copywriter, the CD, and the Sound Engineer. While the Copywriter explains the script to the Voice-Over artiste, the Client, too, arrives.

Scene: A sound room of a huge studio. The Voice-Over artiste is standing behind the microphone. The Copywriter, the CD, Servicing and the Client are sitting around the Sound Engineer who's sitting on the console, taking care of the proceedings.

Client: (*Looking at Sound Engineer's machine*) That looks like a cockpit.

Everybody laughs, programmed to laugh at every joke the Client cracks.

The Sound Engineer plays the track. It's a 30-second Radio Spot.

Smiles all around.

Client: Hmmm . . .

CD: Hmmm . . .

Servicing: Hmmm . . .

Client: I don't like it.

Looks of disbelief.

Client: The voice sounds like it's coming from a guy who has a moustache.

More looks of disbelief.

Client: Play it again.

The Sound Engineer plays the track again.

Client: Yes, certainly, he should sound like a clean-shaven guy.

VO artiste: Well, I am.

The CD, the Copywriter, and Servicing try to calm the VO artiste down.

Client: Do you think he should go and shave?

CD: (*Patting the VO artiste's head*) No, no, that won't be necessary. Just give it another try.

The VO artiste does the Voice Over one more time.

Client: Hmmm . . . No, he doesn't sound comfortable, you know. He sounds like he's wearing an uncomfortable shirt on a beach.

Blank looks.

Client: You know, one of those silk shirts. It's okay if he comes across as wearing a shirt, but he should sound like a guy wearing a *cotton* shirt. And bermudas. Right now it sounds like he's wearing *shorts*.

CD: But shorts are more comfortable than bermudas.

Client: You're right. But that's the point. The comfort level of the voice should be so adjusted that he doesn't sound like a guy wearing a silk shirt on a beach, and who's wearing bermudas, not shorts.

Blank looks.

Client: So, basically, make his upper body a little more comfortable and his lower body a little uncomfortable. Then we'll have it.

The VO artiste does one more version.

Client: Hmm . . . I like it. But I'll tell you what's happening. While the *'Yehi hai right choice, baby'* feel is there; the *'A-HA'* is missing. You know what I mean . . .

Everyone carefully examines their fingernails.

Client: Let's do one more. We're almost there.

Finally, after another version, the VO artiste leaves at 7 pm for another booking.

Client: I think we have enough. Let's just hear the last one.

Sound Engineer plays it.

Client: Hmmm . . . play the one before that.

Sound Engineer gets confused with all the tracks.

Client: Hmm . . . much better. You want to hear the one he did just before lunch?

The track is played.

Client: (*To CD*): What do you think?

CD: I am fine with it, let's go for it.

Client: Wait, I think he sounded much better after lunch . . . play that one.

The track is played.

Seventy takes and eight hours later, the Client still isn't satisfied.

Client: Never mind, play the first track.

Sound Engineer: The first one?

Client: Yes, the very first track.

The track is played.

Client: I think this is the best one we have. What do you think, guys?

Everyone nods without expression.

Client: Cool, let's go with it!*

---

*Every word used here is unfortunately based on a true incident.

TVC

(Writing in full about a TVC, or a television commercial, is beyond the scope of this book, or any book for that matter. Hence, it has been conveniently avoided. *Damn the author!*)

360

The newest, fanciest term to be born in an Agency, probably fathered by a CD whose brain was running on enough beer to send an elephant into *must*, or like any other man with an equal level of inebriation (like the security guard), it means a Campaign that includes each and every medium man, animal and the Yeti can dream up. It is based on the belief that consumers are no longer where the Ad Gurus thought they were, and given that an amount equal to the country's GDP is riding on the campaign, it's imperative to catch the Target Group. (Not even Agency people can justify large budgets for just playing Counter Strike.) The best way to attack a perfectly innocent layman (read TG), wherever, whenever and however possible, is via 360. Places where the consumer spends at least five seconds of their time daily are given preference—which is why you see stickers in toilets, graffiti on hospital ceilings, stands outside morgues, anywhere it's possible to hog the consumer's attention.

Teaser Ads

A Teaser is a form of Campaign where a single Ad isn't clear by itself but builds up curiosity over successive Ads before finally revealing the product/service being advertised.

There is only one reason for the Teaser to be born:

They couldn't come up with an idea for all the Ads in a Campaign the day they were supposed to.

Art Director: Man, I'm stuck.

Copywriter: So am I.

CD: It's okay. I have a solution.

Art Director: What?

CD: How many Ads do we have now?

Copywriter: Two.

CD: And how many do we need?

Copywriter: At least five.

CD: Right. And we don't have any more days.

Unanimously: Yes.

CD: So let's present the Ads we have right now and tell the Client it's a Teaser Campaign. That it's going to build up curiosity. So, while it builds up curiosity, we think of more Ads to complete the Campaign. That way we buy time, meet the deadline. The Client is happy. We are happy. Everybody wins. (Loud noises of agreement are followed by a rare community hug.)

No Copy Ad

This is the type that doesn't contain a single word. It is a visual so strong that it doesn't need any words to complete the communication, the entire message being conveyed by only a picture—e.g. an Ad showing Paris Hilton in the nude, an image calculated to promote engine oil. The Ad works on the premise that the visual itself is so captivating that the reader won't get time or chance or have the inclination, even, to bother with the words. (Newspapers today are adopting this method.)

This sort of Ad arises because:

The Art Director's thinks it below him to let a Copywriter touch his creation.

Art Director: (*Looking scornfully at the Copywriter*)You? *You* will write for this Ad?

Copywriter: Cool. I won't.

Art Director: It's settled then, we go with a No Copy Ad

The Copywriter has passed out before the Ad reaches him.

Art Director: Where's the Copywriter?

Everyone avoids his gaze.

Someone: He's passed out in the bar across the road.

Art Director: Dammit! We have to go with a No Copy Ad!

The Copywriter thinks it below him to write anything for the Ad.

Copywriter: (*Looking scornfully at the Art Director*) This? I have to write for *this*?

Art Director: Cool, don't.

Copywriter: It's settled then, we go with a No Copy Ad.

The Boss sacks the Copywriter just when the Ad is about to reach his desk.

Art Director: Where's the writer?

Boss: I just sacked him.

Art Director: So, what do I do with this Ad?

Boss: (*With an evil smile*) Let's go with a No Copy Ad.

The Art CD doesn't want to share the credit.

Art CD: Great Ad!

Copy CD: A line would make it work better.

Art CD: There's no way you're getting your name on this.

Copy CD: Cool. We'll keep it a No Copy Ad.

There is no team; hence the overworked Art Director has to go ahead with an all-out visual Ad.

Art Director: I have this Ad.

Boss: Good.

Art Director: But I need a Copywriter.

Boss: We don't have a head count.

Art Director: I can't wait for you to hire a writer.

Boss: Don't. Go with a No Copy Ad.

The Copywriter isn't sure of his spelling and can't get his hands on a dictionary, or thinks it's too heavy to pick up.

Art Director: Are you sure that's the spelling?

Copywriter: I don't know. But I can't check. The dictionary is in the library/The dictionary is too heavy.

Art Director: So, what do we do?

Copywriter: Does the Ad work without the headline?

Art Director: Of course.

Copywriter: Cool, go ahead with it then. A No Copy Ad.

The Long Copy Ad

The long copy Ad is the least wanted, least trusted, almost extinct type of Ad. Clients are somehow convinced that nobody reads Ads of more than eight words. The Client thinks people don't read, mainly because they don't. Another reason for the Long Copy Ad not to exist is the person who writes it, the Copywriter. A Long Copy Ad is anywhere from 100 to 15,000 words and a Copywriter usually takes longer to write it than Pluto does to complete a revolution around the Sun. It's a once-in-a lifetime sort of a thing and most Copywriters don't stay long enough in one Agency for that to happen.

There are many reasons the Long Copy Ad started.

The Copywriter is ambitious (low-salaried).
Copywriter: I think I'll write a Long Copy Ad.
CD: Cool. Let's enter it for awards next year.

When an Ad goes into too many drafts.
Boss: How's the Long Copy Ad coming along?
Copywriter: I am on the 736th draft.
Boss: Good, good! How has it shaped up?
Copywriter: I don't know exactly. We've expanded it—from seventy to 5,000 words. Another draft and it will spill over the page!

The Boss wants the Copywriter to be busy.
Boss: What's on your plate?
Copywriter: (*Yawning*) Fish from yesterday's lunch.
Boss: How about writing a Long Copy Ad?

The Copywriter hates the Art Director.
Copywriter: I've written a Long Copy Ad.
Art Director: I don't have time to design it!
Copywriter: The NCD says it'll win us an award, wants to see Layouts tomorrow.
Art Director designs the Ad, using all the text, feeling like a typesetter in a newspaper.

Whenever Long Copy Ads are made, they don't look too good because of various reasons:

The Boss sacks the Art Director just when the Ad is about to reach his desk.
Copywriter: I have a Long Copy Ad!
Boss: I just sacked the Art Director.
Copywriter: So, what do we do?

Boss: Get Studio to design it.

The Art Director is busy checking Proofs.
Copywriter: I have written this Long Copy Ad.
Art Director: I don't have the time.
Copywriter: So, what should we do?
Art Director: Do it yourself.

There is no Team.
Copywriter: I have a Long Copy Ad!
Boss: Good.
Copywriter: But I need an Art Director.
Boss: We don't have a head count. Get Studio to design it.

There is only problem here. The Studio Guy is already taken by some other group which is preparing its Artworks for the same Pitch.

It's presentation time.

Next morning, everyone comes to office as if nothing special is going to happen, going through their usual daily routine: checking mail and playing Hangman and chess. (Secretly each one has his/her Campaigns ready—some with Long Copy Ads, some No Copy Ads, some blank Ads, some scribbles, some generally hanging around, genuinely clueless.)

The NCD walks out of his cabin, drifting into the Creative area to see everyone, serious at work.

NCD: Boys, aren't we supposed to sit on Layouts for the Pitch? Panic spreads and everyone rushes for printouts, some pulling out old Campaigns from their desks and rewriting a new headline over it with a permanent marker. They all assemble in the Conference Room for a presentation before the presentation, again getting ready to:

1. Consume two-thirds of the calories and cholesterol in the world.
2. Play Pictionary.
3. If time permits, present Campaigns.

The NCD rises, taking a deep breath.

NCD: The air smells of promise.

CD 1: It's Domino's.

CD 2: I had a bath today.

CD 3: I washed my hair.

NCD: Brilliant. Just the right spirit, now let's see the Ads.

Campaign after Campaign is presented.

NCD: What was the Brief?

Planning: There was no Brief.

NCD: No Brief?

CDs: That was the Brief. There's no Brief.

NCD: Well, none of the Campaigns are run on the Brief.

After sorting out the confusion over the Brief being no Brief, the NCD speaks again, looking at the presentation of a Campaign.

NCD: The headlines aren't so good.

CD 1: It was the Brief.

NCD: The Layouts aren't so great either.

CD 2: It's the Brief.

NCD: Wait. The logo is wrong too.

CD 3: It's the Brief.

NCD: I think we need a new Brief.

CD 2: But this Brief works so well. It pushes Highstyle to a new level.

NCD: A bird flying in the air with 'Soaring Style' as the headline? You think so?

CDs: It at least breaks the clutter of the category.

NCD: That's true, nobody's done that before.

Self-congratulatory smiles all around.

NCD: The images don't look too great. We need better images.

Art CDs: (*To anyone who's listening*) Do you know any good image sites?

NCD: Get high-res images and let's roll with these (*picking up pieces of Campaigns and pizza from the huge conference room table*). We need everyone in this office to make this Pitch work. The future of the Agency depends on it. It's big revenue. You'll get to make so many Sale Ads, so many offers; this is a high-spending Client. So, everyone, on your toes. We are the people we've been waiting for. Each one has to be a driver. There are no passengers on this journey.

Servicing: (*Whispering*) Does that mean I won't have to drive people around anymore?

CD 2: Maybe he's sacking his chauffer.

Long pause and stares around the table.

As everyone gets up to leave, the NCD speaks again.

NCD: At this crucial time, I'd like everyone to be really charged up and inspired. And what better way to do that than with this presentation I have here, featuring the best Ads in the retail sector.

As the lights are switched off, so are the brain cells. As the lights come on again after what seems like an eternity, everyone is sitting back in their chair wondering what went wrong, some scribbling out their resignation letters on the table.

NCD: We need to do such work that our hands tremble when we present it. Because only when your hands are trembling do you know that you have something special, something phenomenal and something that can change the course of our lives. Let's go for it, boys. Let's meet again next week.

We're in this together. All of us.

ALL OF US
ISN'T AS GOOD
AS ANY OF US.

Here are a few of the types of Creative exiting the conference room:

The Enthusiast aka The Agency Man

This species is usually of the Copywriter variety. The Enthusiasts are the ones who are the heart and soul of the office (who spend most nights in office, 'working') who irritate you at all the worst times: while you're deeply lost in a Layout or while you're checking copy or—if you're a passive Copywriter—in your slumber, which is when they hit you with a football. They are those who watch all the DVDs in the library, who will lunch for at least four hours, whom you look at and wonder, how in the world does he not have any work, EVER!?

But therein lies the trick. They are the ones who come out at the end of the day being congratulated by the NCD for maximum output, leaving you wondering why and how, creating a strong wave of pent-up hatred, making you want to do un-co-worker-like things. But their smiles and grateful acceptance of the laurels bestowed upon them make you forget the whole thing as you go back to your Layout or Artwork and they to their clicking pictures on the boss's fancy I-Mac—which you get to see only when the boss tears apart your Layout, which you sent to him at 3 am before leaving. They are the smooth talkers who're friends with everyone, right from the janitor to the MD, the ones who have a 'setting' with each and every one in the office, who get the extra serving of coconut chutney (which actually isn't such a big draw) and coffee seconds after the canteen guy tells you there's no coffee left.

The 'I-Quit' Quitter aka The One-Agency Man

This is the species that is always ready to quit, who's never happy with what he's doing at any point of the day, (yes, disappointments dog them even in the loo or while having sex). They think they're meant for bigger things, to do better work in a better office and usually at their boss's salary. And, fuelled by such misconceptions, they are always ready to quit. The problem is, they don't.

You: So, how's it going?
The 'I Quit' Quitter: (*Ugly face*) Same shit. Different day.
You: Hmmm . . .
The 'I Quit' Quitter: I am quitting, man . . .
You: Ya? When?
The 'I Quit' Quitter: Soon, man. Gonna show them.
You: I'm sure, man.
The 'I Quit' Quitter: Ya man, they don't deserve me. I'm going, boss.

Eventually, a few months after this conversation (the exact time can't be ascertained because they say this every day), after *you've* quit and moved on to another place, you bump into the same person.

You: Hey, how's it going, man?
The 'I Quit' Quitter: Same shit. Different place.
You: Oh, where are you now?
The 'I Quit' Quitter: I'm still there . . . It just *feels* like a different place.

You: Oh . . .

The 'I Quit' Quitter: But this time, I'm quitting . . .

You: Okay . . .

The 'I Quit' Quitter: Not working for peanuts, man . . .

You: I'm sure, man.

The 'I Quit' Quitter: Ya, man, they don't deserve me. I'm going.

After a few years, you bump into him once again . . .

You: Hey, how you doing, man?

The 'I Quit' Quitter: Same shit. Different place.

You: So what's up?

The 'I Quit' Quitter: Still there . . .

You: Oh . . .

The 'I Quit' Quitter: But I'm quitting now . . .

You: Okay . . .

The 'I Quit' Quitter: I'm too good for them, man . . .

You: Am sure.

The 'I Quit' Quitter: Ya, man, they don't know how lucky they were to have me for as long as they did. I'm off, boss. What about you?

You: Well, that's my kid there . . .

The 'I Quit' Quitter: He's your son? Looks familiar . . .

Your son: I'm a trainee with you.

The 'I Quit' Quitter never quits. Not even saying that he's quitting.

The Comfortably Numb aka The Client's Man

Another variety floating around in an Agency is one who isn't affected by anything at all. He is slowly converted into this state.

Here's the process:

Servicing: The Client wants you to change the backgrcund colour/headline.

Enthusiast: NO WAY! Over my dead body.

After a few years in the Agency:

Servicing: The Client wants you to change the backgro und colour/headline.

Somewhere between Enthusiast and Comfortably Numb: Cɛn I talk to the Client?

Slowly, after the conversion is complete and he has becone Comfortably and completely Numb . . .

Servicing: The Client wants you to change the background colour/headline.

Comfortably Numb: (*Watching TV in the library*) The Layou:'s open on my machine. Change what you want.

Servicing: But I don't know how to operate it.

Comfortably Numb: Just press F11. And follow Help. Oh, ma⁊, The Undertaker choke slammed him!

They are the Client's dream come true because whatever tʰe Client says, they hold it as sacrosanct and do it without further thought, assuming the Client can do all the thinking required (which the Client, too, assumes he can). Nothing affects thʰs variety because they've given up and accepted the fact thɛt it isn't about creativity and that they were fooled into thinkin⊒ so in their growing years.

Servicing: Make the background colour brighter.

CN: Sure (*Cheerfully dragging the mouse*).

Servicing: Change the headline colour.

CN: Sure (*Picking colours and giving 23,209 options.*)

Servicing: Now make the logo bigger.

CN: You got it (*Obediently dragging it out of the Layout*).

Servicing: GOOD! Just, *slightly* smaller.

Servicing: Great! Now burn a CD.

CN: Done (*Pulling out lighter from pocket*).

The Real Quitter aka The Creative man.

Creativity and the rate of quitting are in direct proportion to each other. The ones who think they're really Creative very rarely stick to one place. They're always ready to quit, convinced somehow that they'll do better anywhere but where they are already. And hence, they quit virtually anytime, anywhere—the Conference Room, in the middle of a Briefing—yes, even in the loo.

Scene: Conference Room of a big Ad Agency, meeting in progress.

Real Quitter: (*Getting up suddenly*) How long will the meeting be?

Blank faces.

Real Quitter: That's it, I quit.

The Real Quitter essentially does only one thing: quit. Usually with notice, which he chooses to hang on the handle of his boss's cabin at around 2 am. The only real confusion is the date . . .

CD enters next morning and reads the illegible resignation stuck on his cabin door: 'I QUIT! You won't see me tomorrow.' (Under the note is the time—2 am.)

CD: (*Making a call to The Real-Quitter*): Hello? Hi . . . you said I won't see you from tomorrow.

RQ: Hello?

CD: But you left this note at 2.30 am, which essentially is today.

RQ: Hello?

CD: So when is tomorrow? Today or tomorrow? Because ideally it should be tomorrow since you wrote this note today.

RQ: But I left the note yesterday when I left office.

CD: That's what you think. It was 2.30 at night. That's today.

RQ: Yes. But I did it yesterday.

CD: (*Getting flustered*) You don't understand. You wrote it at 2.30 am which is this morning.

RQ: No, you don't get it, I wrote it last night.

CD: That's nothing but today morning.

RQ: That means even today is tonight.

CD: Yes! YESSSS! They're all the same. You need to be like me, completely lose sense and understanding of time . . .

RQ: So, what's your point?

CD: Come to office today because you wrote this today and the note says tomorrow.

RQ: Hello?

And that's the problem with the Real Quitter. Since they quit whenever their heart desires, clarity of time is never attained, leading to confusion and eventually, quitting.

The Cynic aka Nobody's Man.

Here's the species that acts, talks and walks like the entire Agency's burden is on its mighty shoulders. The Cynics are the ones who are completely disillusioned with, and have no interest in, life whatsoever. They've reached a point in their lives where they often wonder if their father was right when he said, 'Be a lawyer or something dignified.' They are the ones who've lost the plot, and have understood and accepted and are resigned to the fact that there's no such thing as creativity or ideation; that it's all revenue-driven and you are everyone's prostitute. They call their life an 'Existence' and describe change as 'Bending Over'.

And, needless to add, too many players have spoilt the Pitch.

Having worked the entire week through, everyone assembles in the Conference Room on the given day, hoping to get it over with before the Pitch eats into their assigned leave. The NCD walks around the office looking lost while everyone waits for him in the Conference Room looking pretty lost themselves.

Finally, finding nobody anywhere, the NCD walks into the Conference Room for some other meeting that he remembers needing to attend. Seeing everyone already assembled there, the NCD smiles.

NCD: Someone remind me, what are we here for?

CDs: (*Hoping to drop the whole thing themselves*) Nothing in particular.

Planners: Did you know that dodos were our real ancestors?

Servicing: Does anyone need coffee?

NCD: Well, now that we are all here, at least let's discuss *something*. Maybe I should show you a presentation of the World's Best Ads from . . .

CDs: We're here to discuss the Layouts for the Pitch.

NCD: Yes, so, let's see them.

The Enthusiast suddenly gets up, and does a small jig on his chair; the Conference Room resounds with reluctant chuckles broken by the NCD who leans on the table choking on his own drool that has spread freely on the table.

The Cynic: Frankly, do we need more Clients? It means more work. I think we should ideally be going home.

The Real Quitter: (*Standing up*) I quit!

The Cynic: Not now. I meant, every day. We should go early every day.

The I-Quit Quitter: You guys don't deserve someone like me.

The Comfortably Numb: Can we get this over with already?

NCD: On that positive note, let's see the work.

As the Campaigns are rolled out one by one, the NCD looks at each, tilting his head at various angles, making faces, taking deep breaths.

NCD: (*To Head of Planning*) You think they're on the Brief?

Planning Head: There was no Brief. That's the Brief.

NCD: Yes, but still. Do you think the Ads work for the brand and suit its identity, talk to the Target Audience, strike a chord in the people they're meant for?

Planning Head: Well, are you asking me or do you doubt it?

Servicing: Can the logos be bigger in the Layouts?

CDs: They are just dummy Ads right now.

Servicing: So? It still matters.

NCD: (*To Planning Head*) I don't doubt it. I'm just curious. Have we done justice to the Brief?

Planning Head: Considering there was no Brief, I think we may have.

NCD: (*To CDs*) Have we achieved what we set out to do?

CDs: We spoke of many things, what are you referring to? Quitting smoking? Going home early?

NCD: No, no, I meant about the Pitch.

CDs: What did we say? (*Looking at each other in alarm*) Did we commit anything?

NCD: (*Loudly*) We said that we would change everything about the brand!

Loud, unanimous cry: YES!

NCD: (*Louder*): We said we'd break the clutter of the category!

Louder cry: YESSSS!!! .

NCD: (*Voice reaching a crescendo*) And we said we would make a difference!

CDs: (*Exchanging a 'Did we agree to that?' look*) Yes!

NCD: I agree. I think we have a communication that crosses cultures, markets, audiences, sets a trend in the category, breaks the existing clutter of the market, (*voice peaking_* or have we?!!!

Everyone: YESSS!!!

NCD: Great work, boys.

The Enthusiast breaks into another jig.

The Cynic: What's the use of such Creative Ads for the Pitch? We have to go back to doing those Sale Ads again anyway.

The Real Quitter: That's it! I quit.

The Comfortably Numb: Just tell me where the damn logo goes and I'll leave straightaway.

The Cynic: It's no use. Even if we win the Client, what do we get? The same salary, longer working hours and less work satisfaction.

The Enthusiast is still in his jig and introduces a football in the room from nowhere, bouncing it off the wall to provide a sound background score.

NCD: (*To the beat*) Very well, boys. Mount these prints. Dot your 'I's and cross your 'T's.

Servicing: Isn't it 'Tuck in your tees'?

Planning: Get ready to rock. We might create history, without a Brief!

NCD: Yes, boys! However, there's one little thing that has upset me a lot over the past few weeks.

Worried looks around the table.

NCD: While you've done great work for the Pitch and I know you've been busy, that's no excuse.

Worried looks turn into those of wild surmise.

NCD: Don't you want to shine in your careers? Don't you want to be where I am? To feel the rush?

Everyone knows what's coming and that, no matter what they did now, they have no way out of this . . . No, not even blaming their juniors.

NCD: What about those great Ads? What about those larger-than-life-ideas? What about being Proactive?

DECEMBER, 31, 2008.

PROACTIVE

Rs. 2/-

IS A SCAM.

PROACTIVE IS A SCAM | IS A S

PROACTIVE IS A SCAM

There are two types of Ads—the regular ones and the ones done for awards (nicknamed 'Scams'). The former are the ones we see (or probably, miss) dotting our landscapes and filling our newspapers/magazines. Scam Ads aren't usually seen unless you subscribe to *The Free Press Journal*. They aren't released because the Client refuses to pump in money, because he thinks the Ads are too intelligent for the layman to understand. (The Client uses himself as the yardstick for society.) So, for the growth of the Agency (read 'glory of the NCD'), Agencies release these Ads with their own money and enter them for awards. An Agency is deemed good or bad depending upon how well it does 'Scams'. It's not really known when and how or where (probably the Conference Room, but nobody can tell) they came up with this idea but two things are certain:

1. It was a product of a Brainstorm.
2. It was an Offsite.

Q. What exactly is being Proactive?
A. Nobody knows; they're still in the Brainstorm trying to come up with the answer.

Q. How does one become Proactive?
A. By not doing regular work.

Q. Does being Proactive help?
A. Depends on where the Offsite is.

Q. So why is it insisted upon?
A. The NCD needs something to talk about.

Q. Why does an Agency need awards?
A. The NCD needs to travel.

Scene: The NCD and senior CDs are in the Big Conference Room.
NCD: Our jobs aren't satisfactory.
Copywriter and Art Director: Tell us about it!
NCD: Boys, we need to make Ads that make us feel really proud, we need to connect with the Clients more.
CD 2: The MD should get a new wife.
CD 3: We should have a policy to hire only hot trainees.
NCD: Is there a different way?

(*Deeply introspective looks with everyone looking at the table or outside the window.*)

NCD: Boys, everyone's hopes lie on us. They all think we love our jobs . . . Can we make better Ads? Without money, without approvals, just pure intent . . . just for the love of work? The time has come to change the way Advertising works.
CD 1: Does it mean we can go home earlier?
CD 2: And drink?

NCD: From now on, we'll choose Clients and make Ads for them, making our own Brief.
CD 1: (*Interrupting*) That's a good idea. Sack Servicing!
NCD: (*Continuing*) With ideas that inspire us.
CD 2: Like a heavy lunch?
NCD: And, at every meeting, we'll present these Ads to the Client and get him to spend, and aim for those dizzy heights

of success! (*In an advanced state of euphoria*) Let's do more. Let's be PROACTIVE! (*Reaching a climax.*)
CDs: (*Together*) We need more trainees.

And thus was born Proactive—or doing more than what your job expects you to do—making Ads and trying to force them down the Client's throats, getting him to pay for them, somehow releasing them and entering them for prestigious awards.

The idea was to come up with ideas and was gratefully accepted by everyone in the room because it meant:
1. More Brainstorms.
2. More Offsites.
3. More chances to pretend to work by staring at the wall, to come up with ideas but actually reading the phone number of the furniture dealer of the cabinet on the wall over and over again till you start dialling it uncontrollably.

The intent was good; it meant having to think for some time in the day, to come up with ideas. The catch lay in expecting the Client to pay and getting releases. The system firmly in place, every Friday evening everyone was expected to assemble in the Big Conference Room with at least three Campaigns each . . .

Scene: Friday evening. Everyone's in the Conference Room.
NCD: All right, boys, let's see some Ads (*pointing to the first team*).
CD 1: (*Wants to say, 'You know, I was never interested in Scam Ads. I think it's a corruption of a creative mind. People*

are doing it for survival now, just like in the police department, where if you don't take bribes you're left behind. It's all rubbish. Advertising and Design as a craft is much bigger and larger than all this. I enjoy that and really don't care about awards. However, I won't mind coming up with an award-WINNER tomorrow. It's a lucrative business.')

What he actually says: I didn't get the time, but my team sure did.

Team 1: (*Reluctantly arranging the Campaign on the table*) Sir, we didn't get too much time . . . there was a lot of work.

NCD: (*Disgusted*) There will always be work. The choice is ours; do we really want to succeed in life? Do you want to be a name? Do you want to be big? Making these stupid Ads for stupid Clients won't help.

CD 1: (*Interrupting*) Sir . . .

NCD: Let me finish. Clients are banal; they'll never let you do what you want. Are you happy? Ask yourself. Don't you want to feel the rush in your arteries when you get that big winner of an idea?

CD 1: Sir . . .

NCD: Oh, what is it? And who's this, is he a new recruit?

Stranger: I am the Client.

Dead silence in the room with all CDs lunging for their Ads in a desperate effort to hide their faces, the only sounds heard being the hum of the air conditioner and the tramp of the Client's feet marching out of the room.

NCD: Right! So, we need to create time, boys. This is the only way you'll grow. (*To the next group*) Do you have anything?

Other Group: (*Excitedly*) Yes, here!

NCD: (*Seeing a Proactive Layout*) That's a great Ad! But the

Client won't buy it. (*Grim look*) We'll have to release it with our own money.

CD 1: Have you heard about the new personal loans in the market? (*Handing him some pamphlets.*)

NCD: Call Servicing.

Servicing rushes in.

NCD: (*Handing him the same pamphlets*) Get these released, at any cost! There are some good personal loans available.

Servicing: (*Hesitantly*) Sir, there's a new daily called *The Manipur Scoop.*

NCD: (*Ecstatically*) Brilliant! Go for it! See, boys, it's not that difficult. Let's meet again on next Friday. And, *this* time I want everyone to be Proactive.

Scene: Next morning, young, dreamy-eyed Copywriter and Art Director are sitting in the library discussing ideas that will change the world or at least their lives, doing Proactive work. The Creative Director enters.

CD: What are you up to?

Copywriter: (*Enthusiastically*) We're doing Proactive work.

CD: (*In a rage*) What?

Art Director: (*Undeterred*) Proactive. We have some good ideas.

CD: What about that Brief you had?

Together: We'll do that later.

CD: What do you mean later? Where do you think salaries come from? Client work is real work. Work on real Briefs. Who told you you could waste time on this?

Together: (*Confused*) But the NCD . . .

CD: The NCD? Who's your boss?

Together: You.

CD: The NCD is here for personal glorification. You think he cares about you? Do some *real* work. That'll help your career.

Together: (*Disappointed*) But . . .

CD: Nothing doing. Show me Layouts in the evening (*exits*).

As they sit through the afternoon making boring Sale Ads, the NCD happens to pass by.

NCD: What's up boys? Any great ideas? What's this? A Sale Ad? Stop wasting your time.

Together: But . . .

NCD: Don't you want to grow? To be famous? To feel the rush? Does this satisfy you?

Together: But . . .

NCD: This is regular work. But the real joy lies in doing Proactive work.

Together: But . . .

NCD: Nothing doing. Show me Layouts tomorrow (*walks away*).

Next morning, as the Art Director walks in drenched, looking a mess, he bumps into the NCD in the lift. The NCD, who's come in his swanky Mercedes, looks at him in disbelief.

NCD: It's raining?

Art Director just looks at himself from top to toe in reply.

NCD: Is it flooded?

Art Director nods, wiping water off his brow.

NCD: Did you shoot anything?

Art Director: I nearly drowned.

NCD: These are all opportunities. They can be effective Ads.

Art Director: But there are people out there who need help.

NCD: Screw that. Get a camera. Shoot the flooded places. We can just add a logo of one of our Sports Channel clients with a smart headline like ... (*looks upward*) ... Sport is everywhere.

Art Director: But I nearly died.

NCD: Go out there, right now! I sense awards. We might win.

The Art Director, somehow laying his hands on a camera from somewhere, heads out again in the pursuit of an award while the NCD glides into his warm, cozy cabin.

Being Proactive is the best way to be inactive and still get a promotion.

Everyone shifts around nervously in their chairs, looking down, studying the carpet, staring vacant-eyed at the huge Conference Room table, all trying to avoid the NCD's stern gaze and his eternal question.

NCD: Well, does nobody want to be Proactive?

CD 1: We were working all nights and days, even on the weekend.

CD 2: Plus there was the regular work—the Artworks, the Layouts, the Proofs, the changes, it never ends.

CD 3: Plus there was no electricity one evening.

NCD: Where was I?

CD 1: My team was busy, they couldn't have possibly thought of anything.

CD 2: Same here.

NCD: Well, I would like to hear that from the team.

CD 1: They're not here. They have Artworks to take care of.

NCD: What about personal growth, boys?

CD 1: We need higher salaries, that's all.

NCD: What about the rush?

CD 2: I've been constipated for the longest time.

NCD: What about that kick?

CD 3: There's a great new dealer right behind the slums, he even has a cell!

NCD: What about the rush of blood to the head? To taste success, to excel, to prove to the world that you're the best brains there are?

Unanimous: We were more committed to the Pitch.

NCD: Pitch? What Pitch?

CDs: (*Pointing to the printouts*) These.

NCD: Oh yes! It slipped my mind. Yes, boys! We can always be Proactive later, but first, as an Agency (*shouting*) what do we need?

CDs: Leave.

NCD: (*Shouting louder*) To grow, what do we want?

Blank looks.

NCD: We need more business. We need more Clients. WE NEED TO PITCH!

The Pitch wins Clients and Clients provide the money to run Agencies. Does that mean the Pitch is the most important thing for the Agency? So that it can hire the most creative people in the business, function smoothly and prosper? Wrong. It's the location.

The Pitch is a high-level meeting attended by high-level seniors from both sides as everyone back in the Agency enjoys a day of playing Name-Place-Animal-Thing on all the Layouts that the NCD decides to leave behind since they aren't 'good enough'. It starts with all the important people of the Agency assembling early in the morning, dressed in their best, riding to the Client's office in their big cars, hoping to impress him in case he's watching them arrive from the window.

Q. What is the proper way to begin a Pitch?
A. The best way is to prepare numerous Campaigns—possibly 'inspired' by other Campaigns that you think the Client will never get to see in his lifetime—wearing clothes and using items only from Highstyle.

Q. But what if the Client isn't into retail? Airlines, for example?
A. The motto is simple—use what the Client is.

Q. Will the Pitch ever have Ads that normal people (read Clients) will understand?
A. The NCD and CDs are Brainstorming about that.

Q. So this will never happen?
A. Correct.

Q. How many Campaigns should a Pitch have?
A. Preferably at least one more than the last time.

Q. How does the NCD choose the Campaigns?
A. That depends on the hot intern's personal choice of colour.

Q. Why does the NCD make you do so many Campaigns?
A. Because he doesn't like you.

Before the Pitch, the campaigns are presented to the MD/CEO of the Agency since they don't want to appear clueless in the real Pitch, though they actually might be.

Scene: A huge conference room with the NCD, the CDs, the Planning Head, the CSD and the MD. The NCD presents the Campaigns one by one, ably supported by the Planning Head, who throws in facts and figures to please the MD. After a long pause, the MD finally speaks.

MD: Boys, I happened to be in the Creative Department this morning at 9.30 and there was not a soul there.

CD: You should've checked the library; you'd surely have found the Copywriter.

MD: But what about the rest? The official time to begin your day is 9.30. If I can make it, Housekeeping can make it, HR can make it, Security guys can make it, Servicing can make it, why can't anyone in the Creative department? I understand you guys are creative and all that, but discipline matters, guys. You need to set an example.

While the CDs want to protest saying they leave at odd hours, they choose to nod gravely.

MD: It's not just in the morning, but even during the day, if I ask for any of you, the only answer I get is, 'Oh, he's stepped out.' What is 'stepped out', guys? You are accountable to this office, to your profession, to your brands. You can't just 'step out'.

Everyone shifts uncomfortably in their seats.

MD: When I ask how long ago, where you've gone, or how long you'll be, they reply, 'He left some time back, we don't know where; he said he was just stepping out.' I call you on your cell, I get the same thing, 'I've just stepped out. I'll be back some time.' Can we please be more specific about timings?

MD: I also happened to see your desks and cabins. (*Shrugs*) A clean desk is a clean mind, guys.

Everyone groans inwardly.
The MD walks out.

CD 1: Does that mean he liked the Campaigns?
CD 2: I need to call my mother.
CD 3: Maybe we should all be given roll numbers, and identity badges too.
NCD: Great idea. Let's make up naughty designations for everyone. Put someone from your group on that. I think the MD loved the campaigns. I'll see you boys tomorrow.

Finally, next morning, they all assemble at reception with important questions on their mind such as:

Q. Who gets to ride with the NCD?
A. Nobody.

Q. Then why does the hot new intern claim that she is?
A. Duh.

Q. How do they beat the traffic?
A. Duh.

After much ado over nothing, they leave the Agency for the Client's office.

The Client is the reason the entire business of Advertising exists at all. The Client always wants more; he wants his product not just on every shelf, but in every heart, and on everyone's lips. For this, he needs to take it to them, push it down everyone's throats, and make sure they remember his product, see only his product, wherever they go. Who started it all nobody knows; the Client exists in a broad sense, just like the TG in a brief.

Clients are driven by a pledge which they don't merely take, they imbibe it.

The Client Pledge

My brand is my livelihood.
All Servicing are my slaves and all Creative are oversmart.
I love my brand. I am proud of its rich and varied ambiguity.
I shall always strive to be worthy of it and make everyone working on it feel like shit.
I shall loathe and insult all those working on my account. Yes, the CD included.
To my brand, my profession, and my Agency professionals I pledge my devotion.

Whoever started it also left behind an oath passed down generations.

Client Oath: The 19 commandments.

1. I will never make up my mind.
2. I will always give ambiguous feedback.
3. I will always ask for a bigger logo.
4. I will forever ask for a Layout, no matter the time of day or night.
5. I will give no more than a night to an Agency to create an Ad.
6. But I will always take my own sweet time to approve it.
7. I will never like the Ad in the first round.
8. I will always make them do at least twelve rounds.
9. But eventually I shall choose the first round.
10. I will always ask for a brighter colour. Yes, even if it is an obituary.
11. I will insult Servicing endlessly.
12. I will always show the Copywriter and Art Director that I know better.
13. I will keep changing a design till there's nothing left of the original.
14. I will rewrite the headline till the Copywriter is ashamed to call it his Ad.
15. I will always ask for work to be done on a tight budget.
16. And an even tighter deadline, sometimes within minutes.
17. But I will still expect great work.
18. And only I will decide what great work is.
19. Lastly, no matter what, I will always say, 'Good, but could've been better.'

Broadly, there are four types of Client:

The Lots-of-Money Client

This sort of Client gives freedom when it comes to making Ads, not interfering too much in the process of approvals. They have all the money, so they're unafraid to spend, pumping in money for the actual Ads and also buying space in newspapers and hoardings around the city, publicity in malls and suchlike. But, after the Campaign is up and running they decide to get true to their Oath. Servicing gets a call.

Servicing: (*Enthusiastic and happy*) Yes, sir. Did you see the Campaign?

Client: Yes.

Servicing: So, do you like it?

Client: No.

Servicing: But it's up already. All across the city, in many cities.

Client: Yes, I know, but we were thinking, maybe you guys were right.

Servicing: What do you mean?

Client: Maybe the image you had shown earlier was better, after all. Let's change it.

Servicing: (*Gulping*) Now? The hoardings are up, sir.

Client: We don't care. Make sure the new Campaign is up *with* the image I am talking about, latest by tomorrow morning.

Servicing: It's impossible, Sir. We need to print, dispatch, and so many other things.

Client: All right, all right. Tomorrow afternoon.

Line disconnects.

Servicing frantically calls his CSD and the CD.

CSD: What is it?

Servicing: The Client wants to go back to the other image now. And he wants the Campaign up by tomorrow.

CSD: So, get it done.

Line disconnects.

Servicing dials the CD's number, hoping for some sense.

Servicing: Hello?

CD: Hello?

Servicing: The Client wants to go back to the other image now. And he wants the Campaign up by tomorrow.

CD: Hello?

Servicing: I'm serious.

CD: Just ask the Studio Guy to replace the image in all the media. I can't do anything. It's your problem.

Servicing starts running around again, going through the entire process in a state of panic, somehow managing to meet the deadline.

The Pleasing-the-Boss Client

This is the type that will sit and not react at all till the Big Boss does.

Scene: The conference room of a Client's office. The entire team has been assembled. As the Ad is circulated, nobody reacts, looking on stone-faced, merely nodding and passing it on. When the Ad comes to the Big Boss sitting at the centre, they all look in his direction, hoping to catch the smallest twitch on his face. If the boss makes a sour face, they all adopt similar expressions almost immediately, even before the Creative have blinked. If, by the time they tilt their heads back to look at their Big Boss, his expression has changed, they look back at the Creative with versions and degrees of the same expression—the biggest ass-licker sporting the superlative of the expression on the boss's face.

Once the Campaign is approved, Servicing calls the Client

Servicing: Yes, Sir, all the Ads are approved. I will be sending you the media plan by the afternoon. We'll plan where to rent hoardings, which newspapers to advertise in, which channels to play the TV Ad on, and which radio stations to run the Radio Spot on. All based on the TG.

Client: Don't bother. *We'll* send *you* a media plan.

Servicing: Sir?

Client: That's right, by the afternoon.

When such a Client decides the media plan, he does it on the basis of only one thing. No, not the TG, but the boss's residence, the road by which he comes to office, if he's flying in, near the airport, etc. This Client's plan is simple—place it where the boss will see it.

After reading the media plan, Servicing calls the Client.

Servicing: Sir, your product is for college students. But the media you have chosen won't get you to your TG.

Client: That doesn't matter.

Servicing: What do you mean, Sir?

Client: As long as our boss sees it, the Campaign works. Put it up where you've been asked to.

Line disconnects.

The Thinking Client

The Thinking Client is the worst sort. He firmly believes he should've been a Copywriter or a Designer but missed the boat because of the generation he belonged to. As a Client, he fulfils his wish of being Creative to the fullest. He's the kind that lives its Oath at all stages of the Ad. No matter whether he understands it or not, he starts commenting on the Ad, the headline, the background colour, and just about everything else. When the Layout is mailed across, the Client changes it completely, at every stage. And needless to say, the Ad goes through at least thirty stages.

Servicing: Sir, did you see the Ad?

Client: Yes. I don't like the background colour. Make it brighter.

Servicing: Okay.

Client: I have a problem with the headline too. I don't think it works. It needs to be much stronger, more direct. This one is too subtle, doesn't work for my brand image.

Servicing: Um, okay, Sir.

Client: And the image doesn't work either. Make it a little more provocative.

Servicing: Sir, this is just a reference. We'll take care of that in the actual shoot.

Client: What do you mean reference? This is how the final Ad has to look. It *is* going to look EXACTLY like this, right?

Servicing: Well, Sir . . .

Client: Then why are you wasting my time?

Servicing: Sorry, Sir.

Client: Okay, make the changes and send it to me by evening.

As Servicing sends Ad after Ad after Ad, the Client changes everything—the body copy, the address line size, the small legal line, the background colour (yes, again), the font of the headline, the image. After around thirty rounds, Servicing finally calls the Client.

Servicing: Sir, did you see the Ad?

Client: Yes! It's perfect!

Servicing: Well, Sir . . .

Client: See, that's why I love working with you guys. Plan the way forward and mail it to me.

When the actual shoot takes place, the Client changes everything again—the location, the set, the model, the costumes, the props, the photographer, the dates, everything.

Finally, after the final Ad is released, Servicing calls the Client.

Servicing: Sir, did you see the Ad?

Client: Yes, in fact it's in front of me right now and it doesn't look like the Ad I had approved earlier.

Servicing: It's just the same, Sir. The model's changed, that's all.

Client: What do you mean, 'That's all'? The model is the most important element.

Servicing: The earlier one was just a reference, Sir, from the Internet.

Client: Hmm, anyway, I personally think it could've looked much better. Never mind.

Line disconnects.

The Sadistic Client

Actually, this sort of Client is worse than the Thinking Client. While the Thinking Client at least pretends to make sense, the only thing the Sadistic Client is out to do is trouble Creative in every way possible.

Let's say it's an Ad for a popular food chain belonging to the Donald family.

Servicing: Sir, we've sent you the Ad.

Client: Yes, I saw it. I have a problem with the image of the burger there.

Servicing: What, Sir?

Client: The slice of tomato is too thin.

Servicing: I'll look into it, Sir.

After making the slice of tomato thicker, using the wonders of technology, Servicing mails forward the Ad and calls the Client again.

Servicing: Sir, did you see the Ad?

Client: Yes, I still have a problem. The slice of cheese looks too yellow.

(Round 10)

Servicing: Sir, did you see the Ad?

Client: Yes, I don't like those little dots on the bun.

(Round 17)

Servicing: Sir, did you see the Ad?

Client: Yes, but there's that toothpick inserted into the top of the bun. I think the colour of the toothpick should be the colour of our brand.

(Round 33)

Servicing: Sir, did you see the Ad?

Client: Yes, can you make the logo bigger?

(Round 71)

Servicing: Sir, did you see the Ad?

Client: Yes, the burger doesn't look all that fresh, though. Maybe you could brighten it up.

(Round 88)

Servicing: Sir, did you see the Ad?

Client: Yes, the french fries are disturbing, remove them.

Servicing: But *you* insisted on having them, Sir.

Client: Now, remove them. They're disturbing.

It never ends. The Client keeps issuing changes in instalments, one at a time.

Servicing: Sir, did you see the Ad?

Client: Yes, I think it's perfect. Let's release it.

Line disconnects.

The Client always sticks to his Oath and Pledge no matter what. He is very vocal, and is never afraid to express his opinion as long as it fits in with his Oath.

Except at the time of the Pitch.

Finally, the morning dawns. As the big bosses set off with the Pitch—and many versions of it—a strange tension and anxiety creeps into the minds of each of the CDs—'What if the other group's Campaign gets through?' being their primary concern. 'How will it reflect on me? Should I have tried better? Was Dad right; was becoming a lawyer a better option?' In the mean time, the mood is completely the opposite in the office as the juniors roam happily free, grabbing opportunities that the day presents: the cricket bat for example, the remote, and, of course, the sofa in the library. Finally, they can lay their hands on the things they *really* joined Advertising for.

Elsewhere, the NCD looks like he is a man on a mission to the moon, concentrating on nothing in particular, gazing intensely out of his car window.

At this crucial juncture, here are some of the things going through the NCD's mind:

1. Why he has chosen the intern he is riding with.
2. Why he has chosen the car he is riding in.
3. Has he done enough to impress the intern?
4. If the Pitch were to fail, what would be the best excuse he could come up with?
5. Should he arrange for a Brainstorm to come up with an answer to that?

In other cars, the CDs take turns at counting headlights on the highway, debating over why the NCD has chosen to ride with that particular intern, what will happen if the Pitch fails, which was the best way to impress the Client, knowing fully well that their Campaigns won't.

CD 1: I liked that Campaign the NCD left behind.

CD 2: Me too. I wonder what the NCD was thinking.

CD 3: Do you think he deserves to be where he is?

CD 2: What's the difference between him and us?

As they look around for a parking spot while the NCD waits in the lobby leaving the chauffeur to do the parking, they get their answer to that one.

Scene: The really big lobby of the Client's office is absurdly cold; the Agency guys walk in and wait for what seems like a lifetime, playing with their Ads, musing over whether they should strike up a game or two behind them, wondering why they got into all this in the first place, mulling over ways to get out of it, and about life beyond the Pitch.

NCD: All right, boys, this is it! At this crucial juncture I'd like to tell you something someone once said . . . if your hands are not trembling before a presentation, you probably haven't got good Ads.

CD 1: It's probably the air conditioner causing it, but there's no way to tell.

NCD: It's a big Pitch. You know what winning this Client means for us?

CD 1: No.

CSD: A good chair?

CD 2: A day off tomorrow?

CD 3: Free beer?

NCD: It means a bigger car for me, most definitely. A raise, surely.

CSD: You can still get a raise? Is that possible?

Finally, the Client calls them in.

Scene: The absurdly big Conference Room with the air conditioner kept at twelve degrees and falling. The NCD smiles warmly. The CDs take their positions. There are many people representing the Client on the other side of the table. It's like two armies prepared for battle.

NCD: (*Clearing his throat*) We have three Campaigns.

The Client nods.

NCD presents the first Campaign.

NCD: This Campaign shows the evolution of style, showing Ad after Ad, with the Planning head interjecting with a few numbers and slides of his own.

The CDs sit and study the carpet.

The Client nods again.

Head of Planning: As you may be able to tell from the Ads, it was complete freedom for Creative.

The Client still doesn't react.

NCD: (*Pulling out the second Campaign*) In this one, we have a different approach. It's a friendly jab at society and its bad sense of style. Of course, we're not criticising people. We're just saying the obvious in a nice, humorous and friendly way. Of course, it's a Teaser. First, only images will blitz the city to generate curiosity. And once the word spreads, the questions lingering on everyone's minds, we reveal the entire plot. It fits in just beautifully with everything.

The CDs continue staring at the carpet, handing the NCD the Ads as he speaks.

Head of Planning: And of course, research proves that Teasers have worked better if you go through this presentation (*numbers appear on the screen projected from an ultramodern sort of a projector that looks like a stray UFO*).

The CDs now divert their attention to the UFO, taking turns between it and the carpet.

The Client stands as still as the wall, looking just as interested.

The NCD pulls out the third Campaign.

NCD: And this is the last one; here we keep it straight, stylish and sexy. It's just great photography that delivers in a subtle, sophisticated way. It promises large recall value, full of aspiration, modern, understated and elegant.

The Client continues to stand in the same way, arms crossed against his chest, not an iota of emotion on his face.

NCD: Well, that's just about it.

Client: (*Taking a deep breath*) Hmmm . . .

NCD: I think your brand presents us an opportunity to take advertising and your brand to international standards, winning awards and glory. Together, we can change the face of advertising in the country, set new benchmarks and achieve the impossible.

The Client still doesn't move an inch, the expression on his face unchanged. It's like he's not seen anything, nor are there people in the room.

Head of Planning: The Campaigns have promise, they're honest, and they work very hard for your brand, transcending it to a greater height than it is at already.

NCD: It surely breaks the clutter of the category.

The CDs immediately nod in unison, like programmed dolls.

The Client still doesn't give way an inch.

Client: We shall let you know. We have a few more presentations from a few other agencies to go.

The Pitch Report isn't good.

After the actual Pitch, the NCD and CDs resume life as usual. The NCD goes on his official trips in the hope of getting more Clients, hence getting a chance to do more Pitches, in the hope of getting a chance to do an Offsite at his favourite hotel and have more beer and Brainstorms. The Copy CD goes back to challenging people to a game of darts and the Art CD goes looking for more image sites with the standard question to all: 'Do you know any good image sites?'

The Art Director and Copywriter go back to their work—fighting with Studio, sleeping on the library couch, cracking Campaigns, delaying them by promising to sit First Thing Tomorrow Morning. While the trainees go back to sitting in the empty hope that some Brief that someone else thinks below him/her is thrown at them, watching endless television and getting hit by innumerable Briefs (in the form of paper balls) through it all.

Finally one morning, the NCD receives a call from the Client's office.

Within minutes, everyone assembles in the Big Conference Room. A strange sense of excitement hangs in the air because:
1. They think there's free food to be had.
2. Finally, they have a chance to leave their chairs and sit on more comfortable ones.
3. It's another excuse to leave work.

4. It's probably to announce profits and hence a raise.

5. Or maybe, better chairs.

As everyone settles down, the NCD waits patiently, a wide smile on his face as he looks at the future of the Agency before him, at its enthusiastic best.

NCD: Wow! Are there really so many people working here? Where were you guys? I don't see you every day . . .

CD 1: You were on an official trip.

NCD: Ah, correct! Is everyone here?

CD 2: Not everyone. The Copywriter is out to lunch.

CD 1: Servicing needs to go out to a meeting.

CD 3: Do you want to involve Housekeeping in this?

NCD: No, no, this is for Creative.

Servicing gets ready to leave.

NCD: And, of course, for the ones who made this Pitch possible.

CD 1: The Pitch? Which Pitch?

NCD: Highstyle.

CDs: Oh yes, it's been a while we hadn't heard from them. So, is it good news?

NCD: Yes and no.

Incredulous stares around the room.

NCD: Which one do you want to hear first?

CD 1: Is there beer coming?

CD 2: Catch up with me; I will be in the library.

NCD: No, no. Wait, everyone, I won't take long.

Looks of disbelief around the room.

NCD: The Client had called. The news is that . . .

CD 1: I knew it!

CD 2: But he's not said anything . . .

CD 1: Who? The Client?

CD 2: No, the NCD.

NCD: Yes, the Client had called. And they've thought it over.

Planning Head: Out with it already, the wine shop closes in a bit.

NCD: We've won the Pitch!

The Enthusiast does a jig.

The Quitter: I quit!

The Cynic: Oh God, more logos and Sale Ads.

The Real Quitter: I quit, really.

NCD: No, boys, wait, before you get too excited.

CD 1: There's hope?

NCD: Yes. The thing is, though we've won the Pitch, *we've* not really won it.

CD 1: What do you mean?

NCD: The Client has decided to give the account to our Northern Region office.

CD 1: But did they even Pitch?

NCD: No. But the Client believes Creative is better there.

CD 1: So, what does that mean?

NCD: I will be travelling a lot more.

Art Director: Same old Artworks, what else. More late nights.

Copywriter: Can I have the number of the model we used?

CD 2: Does anything change for us?

Servicing: How about better chairs?

Planning: A raise, maybe?

NCD: No, boys, the MD will be talking to you shortly. But the fact remains that the account has gone to our Delhi office.

But, don't lose heart. It's been wonderful Pitching with you.
At this point, I'd like to show you some of the best Campaigns
of the decades gone by . . .

Once again, the lights are switched off.
And so are the brain cells.

The Pitch is over.

That's how it's done in an Ad Agency, yes, any Ad Agency. Advertising is a fun profession that expects you to meet only some basic, simple requirements:

1. An ability to look good unshaven or un-waxed.
2. Being okay with working in recycled underwear.
3. A personality to carry off anything that's unwashed or not ironed, ever.
4. Adept at playing cricket and football with any material in crammed spaces.
5. Versatility, especially when it comes to using paper creatively—as weapons of office war, etc.
6. Adaptability, for times when you have to sleep in a chair if the sofa's taken.
7. Sound communication skills—for when you really need the sofa.
8. Being completely okay with doing everything Daddy said 'No' to—to the point of being proud of it.
9. A knack of looking busy while whiling away time.
10. Being cool—cool being each one's own definition of it—so everything's cool and everyone's cool.

There's nothing better than working in an Ad agency, at least not with your clothes on. The endless nights, the endless presentations and the never-ending chaos—you never stop having fun, not as long as you have the video game or the sofa. Nobody really cares where you come from, what you were doing before; it's an ever-adjusting, friendly environment, so long as you're willing to give up that bat or lend cigarettes around.

It's a place where you never feel like you're working, probably because you aren't, but there's no way to tell. But come what may, it's an industry that's growing by leaps and bounds, with all the money being pumped in by Clients. With globalisation, the playing field is getting bigger (yes, the Agencies have wider corridors and will shortly be introducing LAN games across agencies throughout the world), the opportunities far greater (more sofas in the office), and the scope of growth, endless (but only if you sleep with the right people). As mediums change, the methods change (only 4-over games can be played), but by and large, the industry does and shall remain the same—with a bunch of noisy people who think they can together make a difference, followed by rock 'n' roll all night, and parties every day.

Now, for God's sake, someone hand over that bat.

glossary
should've been at the beginning?

(In Alphabetical Order)

Ad Agency: A place where Advertising work is done. (Ha ha!)

Art Director: Is the one who designs all the Ads. (The Copywriter and Art Director work as a team.)

Artwork: It is the final version of the Proof. Usually, the Copywriter, the Art Director and Servicing sign on the Artwork before it finally goes into printing. This is the final test print—to check for spelling errors, colour corrections, legal lines, etc.

Brainstorm: A session where a group or a team of Creative sit together and discuss ideas to generate more ideas.

Brief, The: The Brief is the basis for making an Ad. It states what the Client wants to achieve with the Campaign/single Ad, the media to be used, the budgets and most importantly, the Unique Selling Proposition (USP) of the product/service—the unique quality of the product which no other can boast of.

Campaign: A Campaign is a series of Ads worked around the same central message—the Brief.

CD: Creative Director; heads a team of Creative.

Copywriter: Is the one who does all the writing: Ads, radio and TV scripts, brochures, etc.

CSD: The Client Servicing Director heads the Servicing team.

Freelance: Is when the Agency hires outsiders for their special talents—at illustration, photography, etc.

Guard Book: A record of all the Ads ever printed and published, for reference.

Layout: It is the design of the piece of communication.

Media Plan: A plan of the mediums to be used for the Campaign.

Media List: The list of mediums and locations (newspaper Ads, hoardings in the city, standees outside theaters) to be used in the Campaign.

NCD: National Creative Director; heads the creative department of all offices of the agency.

Offsite: A special kind of Brainstorm where all the seniors in the Agency meet somewhere outside the office to discuss strategy and come up with ideas.

Pitch: A process in which Agencies present their Campaigns in a bid to win new business in the form of the Client.

Planning: A department in an Agency, it devises the plan, does research and provides Creative with routes to ideas.

Proactive: A popular trend in Ad Agencies; it is work done especially to win awards (sometimes even personal money being pumped into the effort).

Proof: It is the final print of the piece of communication, printed on the actual paper before it is finally produced on a large scale.

Servicing: The link between the Client and Creative. Servicing usually present the Ads (sometimes accompanied by Creative) to the Client, take Briefs, and co-ordinate between the two.

Studio, The: It is a section of the Agency which handles all the nuts and bolts of the final production—from final adapts of sizes to dummies.

TG/TA: Target Group or Target Audience. The set of people the Campaign aims to talk most effectively to.